what's best next

STUDY GUIDE

HOW THE GOSPEL TRANSFORMS THE
WAY YOU GET THINGS DONE

MATT PERMAN

WITH BETH GRAYBILL

ZONDERVAN
REFLECTIVE

ZONDERVAN REFLECTIVE

What's Best Next Study Guide
Copyright © 2019 by Matthew Perman

ISBN 978-0-310-10008-9 (softcover)

ISBN 978-0-310-10014-0 (ebook)

Requests for information should be addressed to:
Zondervan, *3900 Sparks Dr. SE, Grand Rapids, Michigan 49546*

19 20 21 22 23 24 25 26 27 28 29 /LSC/ 20 19 18 17 16 15 14 13 12 11 10 9 8 7 6 5 4 3 2 1

CONTENTS

OF NOTE

The quotations interspersed throughout this study guide are excerpted from *What's Best Next: How the Gospel Transforms the Way You Get Things Done*, and the video study of the same name by Matt Perman. All other resources, including the reflection questions, session introductions, and between-session materials, have been written by Beth Graybill in collaboration with Matt Perman.

A WORD FROM MATT PERMAN

Hello, friend! This study guide and its accompanying video study are a companion learning experience to my book *What's Best Next: How the Gospel Transforms the Way You Get Things Done*. The book contains powerful facts based on years of research, excerpts from literature, and conversations with some of the most inspiring business leaders of our time on why we need a uniquely Christian view on productivity.

You may be here because you are wondering if it's possible to feel less stressed, anxious, and chaotic as you manage your time and get things done. I can tell you with confidence, the answer is yes. If we truly believe the gospel changes everything, then we must embrace the idea that good, balanced productivity practices can also be fueled by the message of the gospel. My aim for this study is, first, to help you reshape the way you think about productivity, and second, to lead you in a practical approach to becoming more effective in your life, with less accompanying stress and frustration. I want to enable you to live the life that God has called you to live with maximum effectiveness and meaning wherever you are.

I invite you in this study to dig deeper into Gospel-Driven Productivity. The practices and methods you learn will provide a helpful and *biblical* pathway to greater productivity and increased personal and professional effectiveness for the good of others and the glory of God. Productivity strategies can be used creatively and confidently in *all areas* of life. So whether you are a student, an executive, a stay-at-home parent, a pastor, a missionary, or a middle-level manager, this study guide is for *you*.

We will begin by looking at why we need to invite God into our productivity, then work our way through principles for living a productive life, exploring a process I call Gospel-Driven Productivity, and, finally, review the results of productivity as we contribute to the greater good of our society and the transformation of the world.

May God give you grace and peace as you seek to grow in your productivity in a way that can keep you oriented and moving forward even when everything around you seems to be falling apart. Join me on the journey of discovering Gospel-Driven Productivity.

FIRST THINGS FIRST

Making God Supreme in Our Productivity

Every Christian must be fully Christian by bringing God into his whole life, not merely into some spiritual realm.
—Dietrich Bonhoeffer

This study is about helping you live the life that God has called you to live, and to live it with maximum effectiveness and meaning. It's about helping you get things done and make ideas happen from a biblical perspective, because most of us feel that we have way too much to do and too little time to do it. And we miss something important and amazing if we don't think about productivity from a specifically biblical perspective. The gospel changes everything— how we go about our home life, work life, church life, community life—everything. So it's important that we know how to get things done and manage ourselves in a way that connects our faith to our everyday work. I want to show you that serving God in the things you do every day and going beyond to engage in God's global purposes—not the life of seeking personal peace, affluence, wealth, or success—is the life of greatest joy and peace. My hope is that this study inspires you to use all that you have, in all areas of life, for the good of others to the glory of God. This is Gospel-Driven Productivity, and this is the most exciting life.

INTRODUCTION

Does God Care?

Have you ever wondered if God actually cares about your work or the way you get things done? Have you grown up thinking that your work week is just that, *your work week*, but the part of life God really cares about is the time you spend at church each weekend? Do you ever wonder if God is even concerned about the fulfillment or lack of fulfillment you are currently experiencing in the work you do?

Here's the truth: God cares about your everyday life—from the weekend to the workplace, whether your workplace is at home with small children, in a classroom, in a church, or in the marketplace. And when you understand or accept that God cares about the work you do, this knowledge has the power to transform your perspective and your practices. Our productivity not only pleases God, it *glorifies* God. When we are productive, we are reflecting God's character and imitating his very own practices.

Remember the creation story? God created the earth and everything in it and then gave the human race something we refer to as the *creation mandate:* "Be fruitful and multiply and fill the earth and subdue it, and have dominion over the fish of the sea and over the birds of the heavens and over every living thing that moves on the earth" (Gen. 1:28 ESV). At the heart of this mandate given by God is the command to be productive and create culture. Adam and Eve went to work right away as they began fulfilling God's commands. They began to grow food (Gen. 4:2), create cities (Gen. 4:17), play musical instruments (Gen. 4:21), and forge tools (Gen. 4:22). They *learned* how to be productive.

If God cared about the musical instruments and tools of the ancient world, then God also cares about the things we create and the tools we use today: our organizational structures, family and team cultures, chore charts, classroom priorities, ministry mantras, church values, music and art, craftsmanship, systems and processes, workflow methods, productivity practices, and so on. Whatever you do in your everyday life is important to God because productivity is important to God.

As you begin this study of *What's Best Next: How the Gospel Transforms the Way You Get Things Done*, it is essential to understand why we need to start with God in our productivity. We often question why it's so hard to get things done, and why the typical answers of efficiency don't seem to work when we consider God's perspective of productivity. But we also see that the ultimate way to be productive from a biblical perspective is to live our lives for God. When we live our lives for God, with the Bible as our guide, then the message of the gospel radically changes our purpose, our manner, our motives, and our foundations. Understanding the gospel enables us to get the right things done in the right way for the right reasons.

If you have been working on the wrong things or getting the wrong things done in the right way, it's never too late to change. The goal of this session is to help you understand what it means to be productive from a biblical perspective, to acknowledge the importance of the things you do every day, and to learn to navigate your workflow in an efficient *and* effective manner that brings glory to God and allows you to better serve others. *This is what matters most.*

THINK ABOUT IT

➤ What makes you feel overwhelmed, overworked, or overloaded these days?

-or-

➤ From your perspective, what keeps us more distracted and less productive in general as a society?

VIDEO TEACHING NOTES

Why Is It so Hard to Get Things Done?

Essence of Knowledge Work: Do and define the work.

The skill of defining our work clearly

> *"The knowledge worker cannot be supervised closely or in detail. He [she] can only be helped. But he must direct himself, and he must direct himself toward performance and contribution, that is, effectiveness."*
> —Peter Drucker, *The Effective Executive*

Effectiveness must be learned.

> *"Effective people have to work at becoming effective. It is a distinct skill that must be learned."*

> **"To be reasonably effective it is not enough for the individual to
> be intelligent, to work hard or to be knowledgeable. Effectiveness
> is something separate, something different."**
> —Peter Drucker, *The Effective Executive*

Two components to work: job skills and the process of how to do work

The "overwhelm" culprits: *overload and ambiguity*

Why Efficiency Is Not the Answer

Efficiency works only when it is secondary, not primary.

More important than efficiency is effectiveness—getting the right things done.

Four things we need to know about efficiency and why it is not the answer:

1. You can get the wrong things done.

2. The quest for efficiency often undermines people—*employees are not cost centers.*

3. Efficiency is often the enemy of innovation.

4. The quest for efficiency often overlooks the importance of intangibles.

> *"Success in the future will be based on the fuzzy intangibles: the culture you nurture, the processes for managing information you set up for your people, the partnerships you form around technology's opportunities and challenges."*
> —Tim Sanders, *Love Is the Killer App*

The "Numerative Bias" by Peters and Waterman

Learn how to identify what is best. *And then translate it into action.*

Efficiency exists so you can serve others better.

Be efficient with things so you can be effective with people.

The answer: Getting the right things done.

How do I know what the right things are?

> *"The aim of time management is the quest for peace of mind. Getting things done with less stress and finding greater fulfillment in what we do."*

Why We Need to Be God-Centered in Our Productivity

> *"My life is full of good things—a nice house, a nice car, a good job, a busy life. But when you asked us to think deeply about our lives, to come to grips with what matters most, it really brought me up short."*
> —Roger Merrill, First Things First

Why are we so often unfulfilled at the end of the day?

> *"The source of our lack of fulfillment is the gap between what is more important to us (personal leadership) and what we are actually doing with our time (personal management)."*

The Four Generations of Time Management by Stephen Covey

1. First Generation: Getting Organized
2. Second Generation: Looking to the Future
3. Third Generation: Identifying Values
4. Fourth Generation: Principles (principle–centered time management)

David Allen: *Getting Things Done*

The fifth generation: from principle-centeredness to God-centeredness

Your center: guidance, security, meaning

Gospel-Driven Productivity happens when God is at the center of our lives.

Why we need to center our lives on God:

1. God is what matters most.

2. We will give an account to God of how we spent our time.

> *"For we will all stand before the judgment seat of God . . .*
> *each of us will give an account of himself to God."*
> **—Romans 14:10, 12 ESV**

3. Excluding God is the ultimate in unproductivity.

> *"What does it profit a man if he gains the whole*
> *world and loses or forfeits himself?"*
> —Luke 9:25 ESV

> *"I am the vine; you are the branches. Whoever abides in me and I in him,*
> *he it is that bears much fruit, for apart from me you can do nothing."*
> —John 15:5 ESV

4. God offers ultimate productivity.

> *"Therefore, my beloved brothers, be steadfast, immovable, always abounding*
> *in the work of the Lord, knowing that in the Lord your labor is not in vain."*
> —1 Corinthians 15:58 ESV

5. God answers our need for fulfillment.

> *"Thou hast made us for thyself, O Lord, and our heart*
> *is restless until it finds its rest in thee."*
> —Augustine of Hippo, *Confessions*

6. The ultimate villain behind all the others: sin

Christ gives us his perfect productivity and life.

Does God Care about Getting Things Done?

Productive versus spiritual

How the gospel does not change the way we get things done:

1. Does God want us to be productive?

2. Does God want us to manage ourselves well?

3. Is there a Christian way to think about productivity?

The first question: Does God want us to be productive?

"Be fruitful and multiply and fill the earth and subdue it, and have dominion over the fish of the sea and over the birds of the heavens and over every living thing that moves on the earth."
—Genesis 1:28 ESV

The parable of the talents (Matt. 25:14–30)

Jesus demands a return on our lives. That's productivity.

In God's power, we develop what he has given us.

The second question: Does God want us to manage ourselves?

"Look carefully then how you walk, not as unwise but as wise, making the best use of the time, because the days are evil. Therefore do not be foolish, but understand what the will of the Lord is."
—Ephesians 5:15–17 ESV

Being wise: Paul refers back to the Wisdom Literature of the Old Testament.

"He who is wise wins souls."
—Proverbs 11:30 NASB

> *"Go to the ant, you sluggard;*
>   *consider its ways and be wise!*
> *It has no commander,*
>   *no overseer or ruler,*
> *yet it stores its provisions in summer*
>   *and gathers its food at harvest."*
> —Proverbs 6:6–8

Two components of effectiveness:

1. Personal leadership

2. Personal management

Wisdom is leading people to Christ and managing ourselves well.

Affirm the good.

The third question: Is there a Christian way to think about productivity?

Faith changes our motives and foundations, but not necessarily our methods.

The gospel radically transforms our motives and foundations.

The beginning of a new definition of productivity

REFLECTION QUESTIONS

1. Have you ever had a season where your work was not clearly defined? Briefly share or write about that experience. What was that like for you?

2. Why do you think it is so hard for us to get things done in general? What keeps you from making the most of your days?

3. Prior to this conversation, how have you viewed the relationship between productivity and the Christian faith, or productivity and the Bible?

4. **Read:** John 15:1–17. How does this passage influence your perspective on a biblical view of productivity?

5. Has there ever been a time when efficiency caused to you be *less* effective, or led you to get the wrong things done, or even make things worse? What did you learn from this experience?

6. What does it look like for you to be efficient *and* effective in your current situation—as a student, a professional, a caregiver, or in ministry?

7. Author Matt Perman mentions three villains of getting things done and determining what's best next: *ambiguity, overload,* and *lack of fulfillment.* Which villain has been the biggest struggle for you, and why?

8. **Read:** Ephesians 5:1–20. How does this passage influence your perspective on a biblical view of time management?

9. What does time management look like for you? What are some ways you strive for peace of mind in your everyday professional and personal lives?

10. Author Matt Perman describes five generations of time management: *getting organized, calendaring and goal-setting, identifying values and connecting goals to those values, principle-centered leadership, and God-centeredness.* How have you moved from being centered on something else—such as money, self, possessions, family, job, church, status—to a God-centered approach to your time management? If you are still in process, where do you need help or support to make this move toward God-centeredness?

Take Action: How will you grow in your ability to get things done? Consider a few next steps you will take to develop the ability to determine what's best next and be productive in your life.

- _____
- _____
- _____

CLOSING PRAYER

- Ask God to help you integrate your idea of productivity and your experience of faith into your everyday work life, whether that's at home, at school, in ministry, or in the marketplace.
- Ask God to give you the courage and the wisdom to make God supreme in your productivity—in your drive for efficiency and effectiveness.
- Pray for the areas in your life where you need the most support and encouragement in the way you spend your time. Ask God to show you a friend who can help hold you accountable in these areas.
- Thank God for caring about our lives as a whole, personally and professionally, and for the Bible as our guide in the way we conduct our lives.

IN BETWEEN SESSIONS

EXERCISE ONE: Clarifying Your Primary Purpose

Personal Reflection

Take time in personal reflection to think about the following questions.

➤ What is the primary purpose of your job right now? Give thought to your answer, whether you are a student, in the workforce, or a stay-at-home parent, and write it down.

➤ Where in your life's primary purpose do you need more clarity? What's unclear to you?

➤ How does your faith in God influence or change the perspective you have on your life's primary purpose, whether you are at home, at school, in ministry, or in the marketplace?

Digging Deeper

Read the following passages and consider how these passages influence your perspective on productivity and purpose.

Read: Matthew 20:20–28

➤ How does Jesus clarify the primary purpose for his disciples in this passage?

➤ What clarifying questions would you have for Jesus about your purpose if you were sitting among the disciples as he shared these words?

Read: Ephesians 2:1–10

➤ How does this passage clarify what it means to be a Christian—one who is made alive in Christ?

➤ What is the primary purpose of us being created as God's workmanship or handiwork?

Personal Action Steps

Consider action steps you can take as a result of what you read today.

➤ What two to three changes or attitude adjustments do you need to make to fully live out your primary purpose with a clear, God-centered perspective?

- _____
- _____
- _____

Reflection and Prayer

Spend a few minutes in quiet personal reflection with God. Pray about whatever is on your mind as you consider your purpose in life. Or use these prayer suggestions as a guide:

- Tell God how you want to live out your purpose with a God-centered perspective. Describe with clarity the life that you want to live, and the way you want to live it—at work, at home, at school, at church—as a result of your personal reflection today. Share your story with God in quiet reflection, by praying out loud, or by journaling your thoughts below.
- Ask God to give you the strength, courage, and perseverance to see your primary purpose from his perspective each and every day.
- Thank God for one or two specific ways he's given you purpose in the work you do.

"It takes more than just enthusiasm, great ideas, native talent,
and hard work to get things done. It takes a method."
—Matt Perman, *What's Best Next*

EXERCISE TWO: Exploring Efficiency and Effectiveness

Personal Reflection

Take time in personal reflection to think about the following questions.

➤ Consider your average workday. Do you focus more on *efficiency* with tasks or *effectiveness* with people in your daily life? If you have a hard time answering this question, consider how people closest to you would answer this question for you.

➤ Why do you think it's easier for you to focus more on the tasks and progress of *efficiency*, or on your *effectiveness* with the people involved in your work?

Digging Deeper

Read the following passages and consider how these passages influence your perspective on efficiency and effectiveness.

Read: Isaiah 32:1–8

➤ Notice the people whose actions are referred to as "wicked" or "evil" in this passage. How are their actions efficient but not effective?

➤ How does this passage describe an effective leader?

Read: Exodus 18

➤ How was Jethro's advice to Moses both *efficient* and *effective*?

➤ What area of your life needs the kind of wise advice Jethro gave to Moses?

Personal Action Steps

Consider action steps you can take as a result of what you read today.

➤ List two to three steps you can take this week to improve your efficiency and be more effective as a leader:

- _____
- _____
- _____

Reflection and Prayer

Spend a few minutes in quiet personal reflection with God. Pray about whatever is on your mind as you consider the concepts of efficiency and effectiveness. Or use these prayer suggestions as a guide:

- Tell God how you want to be more effective and efficient in your own life. Share your specific thoughts, desires, and requests with God in quiet reflection, by praying out loud, or by journaling your thoughts below.
- Ask God to give you a glimpse of what it means to be an effective leader in your current situation or circumstances. And ask God for a "Jethro" who helps you live out this kind of leadership.
- Thank God for one or two specific ways you have been encouraged by this reflection today.

"One of the best places for efficiency is being efficient with things so that you can be effective with people. If you become more efficient with things, you will have more time to give to being effective with people without feeling like you are always behind on your tasks."
—Matt Perman, *What's Best Next*

EXERCISE THREE: What Matters Most

Personal Reflection

Take time in personal reflection to think about the following questions.

➤ How do you determine what matters most? Where do you look to define the things that matter most to you—culture, church, your family, your colleagues, industry standards, school expectations?

➤ How does your relationship with God influence the way you view what matters most? Where is there a "rub" or tension between what matters most to you and what you think matters most to God?

Digging Deeper

Read the following passages and consider how these passages influence your perspective on what matters most.

Read: Ephesians 5:1–20

➤ If determining what matters most means we do "the will of the Lord," then what does this passage tell us about "the will of the Lord"? What is it?

➤ In what ways are you already doing "the will of the Lord" according to this passage? And in what ways do you want to start doing "the will of the Lord" today?

Read: Proverbs 3:1–6

➤ What does the first part of this passage say about what matters most?

➤ How are you *trusting in the Lord with all your heart* and *acknowledging him* in all your ways? Share a few specific examples.

Personal Action Steps

Consider action steps you can take as a result of what you read today.

➤ List two to three specific steps you can take to more fully trust God this week and acknowledge God in all your ways:

- _____
- _____
- _____

Reflection and Prayer

Spend a few minutes in quiet personal reflection with God. Pray about whatever is on your mind as you consider what matters most. Or use these prayer suggestions as a guide:

- Tell God how much you want to focus on what matters most in the work you do. Be specific with your desires and requests.
- Ask God to show you where you are doing the wrong things in the right way, and the right things in the wrong way. Ask God to help you correct these ways.
- Thank God for knowing you and understanding your desire to do what matters most, even when work seems messy or disorganized. Thank God for the grace you have been given to start over again and again.

"When we are getting things done, creating, and making ideas happen, we are not only fulfilling part of God's purpose for us but also reflecting his own character and attributes, which allows us to enjoy his character and attributes in a way that simply observing them does not."
—Matt Perman, *What's Best Next*

EXPLORING ADDITIONAL RESOURCES

Take some time to explore the additional resources recommended in *What's Best Next* session 1:

David Allen, "A New Practice for a New Reality," chapter one in *Getting Things Done*

Peter Drucker, "Effectiveness Can Be Learned," chapter one in *The Effective Executive*

Stephen Covey, "How Many People on Their Deathbed Wish They'd Spent More Time at the Office?" chapter one in *First Things First*

"The Wrong Way to Respond to a Recession": *ttp://www.whatsbestnext.com/2009/03/the-wrong-way-to-respond-to-a-recession/*

"Recessions Are Not for Hunkering Down": *http://www.whatsbestnext.com/2009/01/recessions-are-not-for-hunkering-down/*

Timothy Keller, *Counterfeit Gods: The Empty Promises of Money, Sex, and Power, and the Only Hope That Matters*

Rick Warren, "What Drives Your Life?" Day 3 in *The Purpose Driven Life*

Stephen Covey, "Possible Perceptions Flowing out of Various Centers," "Inside Out," and "Habit 2: Begin with the End in Mind," appendix A, chapter 1, and chapter 3 in *The Seven Habits of Highly Effective People*

John Piper, *Desiring God: Meditations of a Christian Hedonist*

Wayne Grudem, *Business to the Glory of God: The Bible's Teaching on the Moral Goodness of Business*

Leland Ryken, *Redeeming the Time: A Christian Approach to Work and Leisure*

PREPARATION FOR NEXT SESSION

As you reflect on what God is teaching you through this session, read or review part 1: chapters 1–4 of *What's Best Next* by Matt Perman. Also in preparation for your next session, you will want to read part 2: chapters 5–10.

NOTES

GOSPEL-DRIVEN PRODUCTIVITY

A New Way to Look at Getting Things Done

> *Do all the good you can, by all the means you can, in all the*
> *ways you can, in all the places you can, at all the times you*
> *can, to all the people you can, as long as ever you can.*
>
> —John Wesley

INTRODUCTION

What Does God Want?

Living gospel-centered in every aspect of our lives sounds like the right choice to make based on our biblical understanding of God's perspective on productivity. However, you might be asking, *What does it mean for me to be productive in a way that pleases God?* Or, *What does it look like to live a gospel-centered life in the way we approach our personal productivity without rejecting commonsense wisdom or being spiritually weird?* We've already established the fact that to be productive means "to get the right things done," and the right things are the things that God wants done. So to be productive is to accomplish what God wants. *But what does God want done?* God wants us to do good works for the good of others. This is the purpose of productivity.

In order to maximize our productivity from a biblical perspective, there is one underlying principle we must learn: *put the other person first and be on the lookout for ways to do this.* That's it. That is the simple, guiding principle of the Christian life. Putting others first requires love and generosity, and it requires discipline and discernment. It requires understanding the simple fact that we are made right with God by faith alone, not by our good works. And it requires us to be equipped and empowered through prayer and Scripture reading. As we put others first, we must keep in mind that the core principle for making ourselves productive and effective is to know what's important and put it first, rather than being thrown off by the ever-present busyness of life. We must learn to decide what really matters and then *do it*.

In this session, we will see that to be productive in a gospel-centered way is to be abundant in doing good for others while effectively using our individual gifts and abilities. When we learn to develop a gospel-centered method for productivity, we get to be creative, competent, and audacious in doing good for others, both where we are and around the world. It is my hope that you begin to see productivity as a way to make your most loving contribution to the world, as a way to give more than you get, and ultimately as a way to glorify God. This is the foundation of productivity. And when you live with this kind of perspective, you begin asking yourself the core question of productivity: *What's best next?* That question will bring us to Gospel-Centered Productivity as a new way of getting things done with a simple, helpful biblical framework.

THINK ABOUT IT

➤ How do you determine what to do next in your everyday work life?

-or-

➤ How does doing good for others change *them* and change *us*?

VIDEO TEACHING NOTES

Why the Things You Do Every Day Matter

The gospel: *a new way to look at productivity*

What does God want done? *Good works.*

> *"Let your light shine before others, so that they may see your good works and give glory to your Father who is in heaven."*
> —Matthew 5:16 ESV

The purpose of the Christian life: *To do good for others to the glory of God in the light of the gospel.*

> *"For by grace you have been saved through faith; and that not of yourselves, it is the gift of God; not as a result of works, so that no one may boast. For we are His workmanship, created in Christ Jesus for good works, which God prepared beforehand so that we would walk in them."*
> —Ephesians 2:8–10 NASB

> *"[Jesus] gave himself for us to redeem us from all lawlessness and to purify for himself a people for his own possession who are zealous for good works."*
> —Titus 2:14 ESV

> *"You did not choose me, but I chose you and appointed you that you should go and bear fruit and that your fruit should abide."*
> —John 15:16 ESV

The creation and new creation mandate: *We have been doubly created for good works.*

To be productive is to be fruitful in good works.

Where do we do this good?

GTD: David Allen's *Getting Things Done*

Good works: *anything we do in faith*

1. General statements of what God's will is

2. A good work: anything that does good and is done in faith

> **"Knowing that whatever good [thing] anyone does,
> this he will receive back from the Lord."**
> **—Ephesians 6:8 ESV**

Four benefits of better productivity:

1. Reduce the friction in doing good.

2. Amplify your ability to do good.

3. Free up time to serve: a better use of the four-hour work week (from Tim Ferriss's *The Four-Hour Workweek*).

4. Do larger and more challenging good works.

Do the right things in the right ways for the right reasons.

Put Others First: Love as the Guiding Principle for All of Life

Productive: To be abundant in doing good

- How do we do good for others?

- How do we get things done in a way that maximizes our fulfillment?

Guiding principle of productivity: *Put the other person first*. Otherwise known as generosity.

Business research shows generosity and love are better for business.

Love is the guiding principle; generosity is the chief way love manifests itself.

> *"Look carefully then how you walk, not as unwise but as wise, making the best use of the time, because the days are evil. Therefore do not be foolish, but understand what the will of the Lord is."*
> —Ephesians 5:15–17 ESV

Paul's parallel phrases:

- "Walking as a wise person" and "Making the best use of time"

- "Making the best use of time" and "Understanding the will of the Lord"

Jesus wants love.

> *"Love the Lord your God with all your heart and with all your soul and with all your mind . . . [and] love your neighbor as yourself."*
> —Matthew 22:37, 39
>
> *"Therefore be imitators of God, as beloved children. And walk in love, as Christ loved us and gave himself up for us, a fragrant offering and sacrifice to God."*
> —Ephesians 5:1–2 ESV

To be gospel-centered:

- To have Christ first

- To have an emphasis on love

How do we apply love to the workplace?

1. Have good will toward the other person—*motives count.*

> *"Some indeed preach Christ from envy and rivalry, but others from good will. The latter do it out of love."*
> —Philippians 1:15–16 ESV

2. The welfare of the other is your chief concern. *Think hard about what the other person needs, and do that.*

3. Be proactive in doing good, not reactive.

[A loving person is] *"quick-sighted to discern the needs of others."*
—Jonathan Edwards, *Charity and Its Fruits*

4. Be creative and competent in doing good.

"He also who is slack in his work is brother to him who destroys."
—Proverbs 18:9 NASB

We are to do good so God gets the glory.

Do your work as an offering to God.

Your whole life can be filled with worship.

"What is given, is given to that which the individual makes his great end in giving. If his end be only himself, then it is given only to himself, and not to God; and if his aim be his own honor or ease, or worldly profit, then the gift is but an offering to these things. The gift is an offering to him to whom the giver's heart devotes, and for whom he designs it."
—Jonathan Edwards, *The Duty of Christian Charity to the Poor*

The incredible, surprising result of living a life for the good of others:

How the Gospel Makes Us Productive

Justification is at the core of the gospel.

> *"He [William Wilberforce] lacked time for half the good works in his mind"* and *"factories did not spring up more rapidly in Leeds and Manchester than schemes of benevolence beneath his roof."*
> —John Piper, *The Roots of Endurance*
>
> *"The article by which the church stands or falls."*
> —Martin Luther
>
> *"The main hinge on which religion turns."*
> —John Calvin

Justification means:

1. Our sins are forgiven.

> *"Blessed are those whose lawless deeds have been forgiven, and whose sins have been covered."*
> —Romans 4:7 NASB

2. God credits to us the righteousness of Christ.

> *"Just as David also speaks of the blessing on the man to whom God credits righteousness apart from works."*
> —Romans 4:6 NASB
>
> *"But to the one who does not work, but believes in Him who justifies the ungodly, his faith is credited as righteousness."*
> —Romans 4:5 NASB

The chief thing in Christianity is fellowship with God and his people.

The only way to become good is to realize God accepts you apart from your goodness.

> *"But when the goodness and loving kindness of God our Savior appeared, he saved us, not because of works done by us in righteousness, but according to his own mercy, by the washing of regeneration and renewal of the Holy Spirit, whom he poured out on us richly through Jesus Christ our Savior, so that being justified by his grace we might become heirs according to the hope of eternal life. The saying is trustworthy, and I want you to insist on these things, so that those who have believed in God may be careful to devote themselves to good works. These things are excellent and profitable for people."*
> —Titus 3:4–8 ESV

What leads us to doing good?

Why does the doctrine of justification lead to radical action for good? *Because doctrine fuels the joy that empowers obedience.*

> "All these, their several errors, naturally result from the mistaken conception entertained of the fundamental principles of Christianity. They consider not that Christianity is a scheme 'for justifying the ungodly,' by Christ's dying for them 'when yet sinners,' a scheme for 'reconciling us to God—when enemies'; and for making the fruits of holiness the effects, not the cause, of our being justified and reconciled."
> —William Wilberforce, *A Practical View of Christianity*
>
> "The bulk of Christians in [Wilberforce's] day were nominal, he observed, and what was the root difference between the nominal and the real? It was this: The nominal pursued morality without first relying utterly on the free gift of justification and reconciliation by faith alone based on Christ's blood and righteousness."
> —John Piper, *The Roots of Endurance*
>
> "He who is forgiven little, loves little."
> —Luke 7:47 NASB

Peace of Mind without Having to Keep Everything under Control

The trap: basing our daily peace of mind on our to-do list, *which kills our joy and freedom*

The ultimate peace of mind comes through *faith.*

GTD: David Allen's *Getting Things Done* and "Mind like water"

> *"Do not be anxious about anything, but in everything by prayer and supplication with thanksgiving let your requests be made known to God. And the peace of God, which surpasses all understanding, will guard your hearts and your minds in Christ Jesus."*
> —Philippians 4:6–7 ESV

What do GTD and Philippians have in common?

1. Both concern peace of mind.

2. Both deal with anxiety in similar ways: externalize our concerns.

3. Both advocate being comprehensive.

What is the significant difference?

Trusted system versus trusted God

God's peace is not based on our own efforts.

Peace comes first, not second (2 Cor. 2:13).

> *"Work out your own salvation . . . for it is God who works in you."*
> —**Philippians 2:12–13 ESV**

We become free to serve.

Your identity is in Christ.

The Role of Prayer and the Scriptures in Our Productivity

Stephen Covey's *The Seven Habits of Highly Effective People*

Success literature: shift from character to technique.

Os Guinness's *Character Counts*

> "Whereas a combination of faith, character and virtue was the
> rock on which traditional leadership was founded, each of these
> components has crumbled in the twentieth century."
> —Os Guinness, *Character Counts: Leadership Qualities in
> Washington, Wilberforce, Lincoln, and Solzhenitsyn*

The Personality Ethic versus The Character Ethic:

- Personality Ethic: *looks at externals*

- Character Ethic: *looks first at who you are*

Distinction between primary and secondary greatness:

- Primary greatness: *goodness of character*

- Secondary greatness: *being publicly recognized*

> "Private victory precedes public victory."
> —Stephen Covey, *The Seven Habits of Highly Effective People*

You must be a virtuous person before you can really do good.

> *"He is like a tree planted by streams of water that yields its fruit in its season, and its leaf does not wither."*
> —Psalm 1:3 ESV
>
> *"For if these qualities are yours and are increasing, they keep you from being ineffective or unfruitful in the knowledge of our Lord Jesus Christ."*
> —2 Peter 1:8 ESV

Character is at the heart of what God requires: *an intrinsic good.*

Character enables us to discern *what's best next.*

Should we always trust our intuition?

The Golden Rule is the guiding principle for being productive.

> *"It is my prayer that your love may abound more and more, with knowledge and all discernment, so that you may approve what is excellent."*
> —Philippians 1:9–10 ESV

God shapes our character through:

- Scripture—*every day* (Psalm 1)

- Prayer—*every day* (John 15)

The Sermon on the Mount (Matthew 5) connects the Golden Rule and prayer.

God is eager to answer prayer; *therefore*, treat others as you want to be treated.

The Core Principles for Making Yourself Effective

Understand the core concept of the subject.

The Golden Rule: *Do unto others as you would have them do unto you.*

Jesus: *"Love others as I have loved you."*

The Process for Productivity: Know what's most important and put it first.

> **"Organize and execute around the right priorities."**
> **—Stephen Covey, First Things First**
>
> **"The secret of effectiveness is to know what really counts, then do what really counts, and not worry about the rest."**
> **—Rick Warren, The Purpose Driven Church**
>
> **"If there is any one 'secret' of effectiveness, it is concentration. Effective executives do first things first and they do one thing at a time."**
> **—Peter Drucker**

Stephen Covey, *First Things First*, on "Putting the big rocks in first"

The jar: rocks, gravel, sand, and water
   (Draw your own version of this illustration here, if it's helpful.)

The lesson of the jar: the big rocks go in the jar *first.*

Know what is important and do it first.

Gospel-Driven Productivity: The Four-Step Process

1. DEFINE: Know your mission, vision, and roles.

2. ARCHITECT: Weave these things into your life with a flexible schedule.

3. REDUCE: Get rid of the things that do not fit.

4. EXECUTE: Make things happen every day.

Use your productivity for God and others *with a sense of adventure.*

REFLECTION QUESTIONS

1. How has this session influenced your perspective on productivity?

2. Use your own words to describe why God cares about productivity in your everyday life. How does this change your outlook on the work you do at home, in the classroom, or at the office?

3. What does it look like for you to be a productive person? How do you contribute to the greater good of humanity and glorify God by being productive?

4. **Read:** Jeremiah 29:1–14. How does this passage reflect the peace and prosperity of productivity for the Israelites who were in exile?

5. Why do you think so many Christians separate the idea of productivity from what it means to be "spiritual"?

6. **Read:** Matthew 5:16. What does this passage say about what God wants from us?

7. Good works can be described in general as "anything we do in faith," and they can be lived out in very specific expressions in our everyday lives, such as parenting, or neighboring, or working, or ministering. What are some *general* and *specific* ways you do good works?

8. Why do you think we tend to be more *reactive* than *proactive* in doing good for others?

9. How would you describe what it means to be gospel-driven in our day-to-day actions?

10. How will your neighbors, family members, classmates, or coworkers benefit from you practicing a gospel-centered approach to life and doing *what's best next* this week?

Take Action: How can you do good for others this week as an expression of the highest form of productivity: doing good for others in order to glorify God? Think about one or two actions you can take, and then *do them*.

- _____
- _____
- _____

CLOSING PRAYER

- Ask God to help you see clearly how the things you do every day actually matter.
- Ask God to give you the confidence and security to put others first on a regular basis as an act of glorifying God.
- Pray for the areas in your life where you need the most support and encouragement in loving others and in being productive. Ask God to show you who needs your life, and which areas of your life need the most productivity.
- Thank God for providing a biblical perspective and gospel-centered approach to the way you get things done, allowing you to flourish as a creative, courageous human being.

IN BETWEEN SESSIONS

EXERCISE ONE: Every Day Matters

Personal Reflection

Take time in personal reflection to think about the following questions.

➤ What kind of "good" have you done for others?

➤ What makes it hard for you to put others first in life—at work, home, school, ministry, or church?

➤ Which of the three characteristics of gospel-driven Christians do you reflect the most? Which one do you need to work on the most?

Digging Deeper

Read the following passages and consider how these passages influence your perspective on productivity and purpose.

Read: Mark 12:28–34

➤ How does Jesus establish love as a guiding principle in this passage?

➤ What kind of glory does God get as a result of the words and actions of Jesus in this passage?

Read: 1 Peter 2:1–17

➤ What stands out to you in this passage?

➤ What steps will you take to live a gospel-driven life as a result of these inspiring words written by Peter?

Personal Action Steps

Consider action steps you can take as a result of what you read today.

➤ The mark of a godly life is a life that does good *with* God, not one that does good *without* God. What specific actions will you take today to do good *with* God for the benefit of others?

- _____
- _____
- _____

Reflection and Prayer

Spend a few minutes in quiet personal reflection with God. Pray about whatever is on your mind as you consider the biblical perspective and purpose of productivity. Or use these prayer suggestions as a guide:

- Tell God how you want to love others and be more productive in the way you get things done. Ask him to help you desire to glorify him more than you desire your own praise.
- Ask God to deepen your understanding of what he wants you to do in your everyday life as you love God, love others, and contribute to the greater good of the world with your productivity.
- Thank God for two or three specific ways he's gifted you to contribute to the world around you with your creativity, your perspective, and your talents.

_____
_____
_____
_____
_____
_____
_____
_____
_____
_____
_____
_____
_____
_____
_____

> *"The activities of our everyday lives are not separate from the good works that God has called us to. They are themselves part of the good works that God created for us in Christ. And, therefore, they have great meaning."*
> —Matt Perman, *What's Best Next*

EXERCISE TWO: Productivity, Love, and the Gospel

Personal Reflection

Take time in personal reflection to think about the following questions.

➤ If the overarching principle of the Christian life is that we are here to serve others in love and, in doing so, give glory to God, what does this mean for you? How does this rearrange your priorities and your productivity?

➤ Why do you think we so often separate our work world from our personal life when it comes to loving others? How does the insight you gained during this session help you integrate the way you love others at home and in the work you do?

Digging Deeper

Read the following passages and consider how these passages influence your perspective on gospel-centered love in productivity.

Read: Ephesians 5:1–17

➤ What does it mean for you to live as a "child of the light" in your current context?

➤ How are you making the most of every opportunity in your current context?

Read: Titus 3:1–8

➤ How does this passage reflect what God did for us regarding salvation and justification—setting things right with God?

➤ If the gospel is about what God did for us and not what we do for God, what motivates you to do good works for God?

Personal Action Steps

Consider action steps you can take as a result of what you read today.

➤ Are there two or three steps you can take this week to improve your productivity as a way of loving God and loving others?

- _____
- _____
- _____

Reflection and Prayer

Spend a few minutes in quiet personal reflection with God. Pray about whatever is on your mind as you consider the concepts of love and Gospel-Centered Productivity. Or use these prayer suggestions as a guide:

- Tell God how you want to be more productive in your everyday life not because you have to earn your salvation but because you *don't* have to earn anything from him.
- Ask God to help you be more productive as a leader by anchoring your day in prayer and Scripture reading. If this is a new discipline for you, talk to God about what this rhythm could look like, and ask God for the commitment to turn these practices into daily habits.
- Thank God for one or two specific ways you have been inspired or given more freedom by this reflection today.

_____

_____

_____

_____

_____

_____

_____

_____

_____

_____

_____

_____

> *"Love is the guiding principle of the Christian life, and generosity is the chief way love manifests itself in the world of work, our communities, and society."*
> —Matt Perman, *What's Best Next*

EXERCISE THREE: What's Best Next?

Personal Reflection

Take time in personal reflection to think about the following questions.

➤ How do you determine what's best next in your life and in your workflow?

➤ How has this session on why the things you do every day matter most, and how love goes hand in hand with Gospel-Driven Productivity, helped you determine what's best next?

Gospel-Driven Productivity:
1. *Define:* Know your mission, vision, and roles.
2. *Architect:* Weave these things into your life through a flexible schedule.
3. *Reduce:* Get rid of the things that don't fit.
4. *Execute:* Make things happen every day.

Digging Deeper

Read the following passages and consider how these passages influence your perspective on what's best next.

Read: Matthew 6:25–34

➤ According to this passage, what is most important in life from God's perspective?

➤ How do you think you "seek the kingdom first" in your everyday life? What does this look like for you in your specific situation?

Read: Matthew 23:23–24

➤ What does Jesus declare as most important in this passage?

➤ When or how have you been like these Pharisees, ignoring the most important pieces of work and productivity while paying attention to the less important pieces?

Personal Action Steps

Consider action steps you can take as a result of what you read today.

➤ Consider the illustration Matt Perman uses from Stephen Covey's book *First Things First* (also in *What's Best Next*, page 134). First, you have a big jar that represents your life. Next, you have big rocks that represent your major priorities, gravel that represents small priorities, sand that represents other necessities in life, and water that represents everything else in your life. If you fill your jar with water or sand or gravel first, there is very little room left over for the big rocks. So you need to start by filling your jar with the big rocks—your first priorities—so everything else can slide in between those rocks. Can you picture it? Now consider your own life with this illustration. List the top three to five priorities that represent the "big rocks" in your life:

- _____
- _____
- _____
- _____
- _____

Remember that everything else is gravel, sand, or water. The big rocks must come first if you're going to fit everything necessary into your life.

Reflection and Prayer

Spend a few minutes in quiet personal reflection with God. Pray about whatever is on your mind as you consider what's best next. Or use these prayer suggestions as a guide:

- Tell God how much you want to live out the idea and methods of Gospel-Driven Productivity.
- Ask God to show you what's best next in the big things as well as the small things you face this week.
- Thank God for knowing you and understanding your desire to do what's best next, even when you are unsure of what step to take. Ask God to direct your actions and your thoughts as you decide what matters most this week.

_____
_____
_____
_____
_____
_____
_____
_____
_____
_____
_____

"Don't prioritize your schedule; schedule your priorities."
—Stephen Covey

EXPLORING ADDITIONAL RESOURCES

Take some time to explore the additional resources recommended in *What's Best Next* session 2:

Tim Sanders, *Love Is the Killer App*

Keith Ferrazzi, *Never Eat Alone*

Stephen Covey, "Seek First to Understand, Then to be Understood," Habit 5 in *The Seven Habits of Highly Effective People*

Jonathan Edwards, "Love Is Cheerful and Free in Doing Good" and "The Spirit of Charity the Opposite of a Selfish Spirit," lectures 5 and 8 in *Charity and Its Fruits*

J. Douglas Holladay, "A Life of Significance," and John Pollock, "A Man Who Changed the Times," in *Character Counts: Leadership Qualities in Washington, Wilberforce, Lincoln, and Solzhenitsyn*

John Pollock, *Wilberforce*

Robert Isaac Wilberforce and Samuel Wilberforce, *The Life of William Wilberforce*

John Piper, "William Wilberforce: 'Peculiar Doctrines,' Spiritual Delight, and the Politics of Slavery," in *The Roots of Endurance: Invincible Perseverance in the Lives of John Newton, Charles Simeon, and William Wilberforce*

Michael Wittmer, *Don't Stop Believing: Why Living Like Jesus Isn't Enough*

Keven DeYoung and Ted Kluck, *Why We're Not Emergent: By Two Guys Who Should Be*

John Piper, *The Pleasures of God*

James Buchanan, *The Doctrine of Justification*

John Owen, *The Doctrine of Justification by Faith through the Imputation of the Righteousness of Christ Explained, Confirmed and Vindicated*

Jonathan Edwards, "Justification by Faith Alone," in *The Works of Jonathan Edwards*

John Piper, *Counted Righteous in Christ*

PREPARATION FOR NEXT SESSION

As you reflect on what God is teaching you through this session, read or review part 2: chapters 5–10 of *What's Best Next* by Matt Perman. Also in preparation for your next session, you will want to read part 3: chapters 11–13.

NOTES

DEFINE

Know What's Most Important

To every person there comes in their lifetime that special moment when you are figuratively tapped on the shoulder and offered the chance to do a very special thing, unique to you and your talents. What a tragedy if that moment finds you unprepared or unqualified for work which could have been your finest hour.

—Winston Churchill

INTRODUCTION

Defining What's Most Important

It's fair to say that we often look to outside sources for leadership in our lives. Now more than ever, we have easy access to the latest books, podcasts, and video episodes on goal setting, budgeting, parenting, leading, managing, developing confidence, and so on. But what if you knew that you've already been given everything you need for your own personal leadership and management? God cares about where you are going and how you will get there; that's why he gave us Scriptures that speak so clearly to our need to determine what the right things are (personal leadership) and how to put them into practice (personal management). External resources are helpful to our growth and development, but God's Word lays the *foundation* of what it means to lead and manage our own lives.

We've already established in previous sessions that determining the right things to do brings us to the heart of productivity: *doing good for others according to our gifts and abilities in order to glorify God.* Living out this definition of productivity by asking *"What's best next?"* shows good personal leadership. Gospel-Driven Productivity is, therefore, a tool to equip you and enable you to continue putting the right kind of productivity into practice. GDP is the process by which you take your talents, abilities, and opportunities and joyfully make them useful for the good of others and the glory of God.

The first step in achieving Gospel-Centered Productivity is to *define* your mission, vision, and roles. In doing so, you will articulate why you are here at all (your purpose) and what is most important (your life goals). We will cover the basics of this step over the next few pages. However, for a more in-depth look at the exercises helpful to *define*, read part 3 (chapters 11–13) in *What's Best Next*.

THINK ABOUT IT

➤ What is the most important thing you want to accomplish in your life?

–or–

➤ Do you already have a mission for your life? If so, what is it?

VIDEO TEACHING NOTES

What's Your Mission? How Not to Waste Your Life

The three components of a personal mission statement:

1. Core purpose

2. Core principles

3. Core beliefs

You need to first answer: *Who am I?*

The purpose of a mission statement is to define your "rock-bottom" principles.

Life goal or life vision: *What you are going to do specifically with your life*

William Wilberforce

Mission: Glorify God and enjoy him forever.
Life Goal: Bring an end to the slave trade.

You can fail at your life goal and still succeed at your life mission.

Why do most mission statements fail? You can have the wrong mission in life.

God created you and defined your purpose; your role is to know what that purpose is.

> *"Trust in the LORD with all your heart,*
> *and do not lean on your own understanding.*
> *In all your ways acknowledge him,*
> *and he will make straight your paths."*
> —Proverbs 3:5–6 ESV

Creating your personal mission statement:

1. Core purpose: *Overall reason for existence*

> "Let your light shine before others, so that they may see your good works and give glory to your Father who is in heaven."
> —Matthew 5:16 ESV
>
> "God created me—and you—to live with a single, all-embracing, all-transforming passion—namely, a passion to glorify God by enjoying and displaying his supreme excellence in all the spheres of life."
> —John Piper, Don't Waste Your Life
>
> "We inspire the world by meeting the needs of people with content that promotes biblical principles and honors Jesus Christ."
> —HarperCollins Christian Publishing, Mission Statement

2. Core principles: *Guiding principles*

-   What are my main principles?

-   What are my values?

-   What are the values of your organization?

- How do you identify your core principles?

- Would you hold to your core principles even if you were punished for them?

3. Core beliefs: *The foundation of your mission is what God has done for you in Christ.*

Include justice and mercy in your personal mission statement.

"He has told you, O man, what is good; and what does the Lᴏʀᴅ require of you but to do justice, and to love [mercy], and to walk humbly with your God?"
—Micah 6:8 ESV

"The weightier matters of the law: justice and mercy and faithfulness."
—Matthew 23:23 ESV

"He judged the cause of the poor and needy; then it was well. Is not this to know me?"
—Jeremiah 22:16 ESV

Justice means "to use any influence and ability you have on behalf of those in need."
—Gary Haugen, *Good News About Injustice*

"Cease to do evil, learn to do good; seek justice, correct oppression; bring justice to the fatherless, plead the widow's cause."
—Isaiah 1:16–17 ESV

Be diligent and proactive to do mercy.

"He judged the cause of the poor and needy;
then it was well.
Is not this to know me?"
—Jeremiah 22:16

"Resolved, that I will do whatsoever I think to be most to God's glory, and
my own good, profit and pleasure, to the whole of my duration, without any
consideration of the time, whether now, or never so many myriads of ages hence.

"Resolved to do whatever I think to be my duty and most for the good
and advantage of mankind in general. Resolved to do this, whatever
difficulties I meet with, how many and how great so ever.

"Resolved, to live with all my might while I do live.

"Resolved, to endeavor to obtain for myself as much happiness, in the other world,
as I possibly can, with all the power, might, vigor, vehemence, yea violence, I am
capable of, or can bring myself to exert, in any way that can be thought of.

"Resolved, when I think of any theorem in divinity to be solved, immediately
to do what I can towards solving it, if circumstances don't hinder.

"Resolved to be endeavoring to find out fit objects of charity and liberality."
—Jonathan Edwards

Finding Your Life Calling

Know your mission before your goal.

> "Old Palace Yard, London, October 25, 1787: A slight young man sat at his oak desk in the second-floor library. The young man would begin this day as was his custom, with a time of personal prayer and Scripture reading. But his thoughts kept returning to the pamphlets on slave trade that were scattered across his desk. Something inside him—that insistent conviction he'd felt before—was telling him that all that had happened in his life had been for a purpose, preparing him to meet that barbaric evil head-on. . . . He thought about his conversion and his calling. Had God saved him only to rescue his own soul from hell? He could not accept that. If Christianity was true and meaningful, it must not only save but serve. Wilberforce dipped his pen into the inkwell: 'Almighty God has set before me two great objectives,' he wrote, his heart suddenly pumping with passion, 'the abolition of the slave trade and the reformation of manners.'"
>
> —Charles Colson on William Wilberforce, *A Practical View on Christianity*

Your life goal is something that you feel compelled to do.

More accounts of the life of William Wilberforce:

John Pollock's *Character Counts*
Samuel Wilberforce's *The Life of William Wilberforce*
Eric Metaxas's *Amazing Grace*

How do you identify your own life goal? By asking:

1. What would I do if I had all the money I needed and could do whatever I wanted?

2. What would I do if I could do only one thing in the next three years?

Making your life goal happen:

1. Put it where you will remember and review it—*create a document.*

2. Weave your life goal into the structure of your life.

3. Utilize evolutionary progress rather than scripting everything out.

Clarifying Your Roles

A new way to think about your roles: *Roles and the Christian doctrine of vocation*

Role: *An area of responsibility*

The Bible: *Roles are callings given to us by God to serve God and others.*

1. All Christians have a calling—*1 Corinthians 7:17–24.*

> "A cobbler, a smith, a farmer, each has the work and office of his trade, and yet they are all alike consecrated priests and bishops, and every one by means of his own work or office must benefit and serve every other, that in this way many kinds of work may be done for the bodily and spiritual welfare of the community, even as all the members of the body serve one another."
> —Martin Luther, *An Open Letter to the Christian Nobility*

2. Every area of our lives is a calling.

   • Our chief calling is to follow Christ. Then there are secondary callings.

3. Every job and area of life has dignity and meaning.

4. Each role is a stewardship before God.

How to define your roles (vocations):

   List what comes to mind:

The problem: We have a lot of roles.

How do we solve this problem as we think about our roles?

1. Combine roles.

2. Organize (or group) roles.

Four roles influenced by Luther's estates (Luke 3:10–14):

- Family
- Church
- Social
- Common order of Christian love

> *"Feed the hungry and give drink to the thirsty, forgive enemies, pray for all men*
> *on earth and do good to all people everywhere, as we have opportunity."*
> **—Martin Luther (also Galatians 6:10)**

Five areas according to Matt Perman:

- Individual
- Family
- Church
- Social
- Professional

Role-mapping: *Where do you map out these roles?*

1. Use your mission document.

2. Use a note-keeping program—*or mind-mapping tool.*

3. Minimize the annoyance factor.

4. Create role plans—*how to improve any role.*

Role-mapping—*how to stay focused and keep going*

1. Review in weekly planning.

2. Identify what you have to keep in motion with weekly structure.

REFLECTION QUESTIONS

1. How has this session influenced your perspective on the *most important thing* in your life?

2. We often skip ahead in life by asking, *"What am I going to do with my life?"* when, instead, we should be asking, *"Who am I, what do I stand for, and why am I here at all?"* How would you answer these questions?

   • Who am I?

   • What do I stand for?

   • Why am I here at all?

3. As you read your answers to the questions above, is there a personal mission statement that stands out to you or comes to mind? If so, share it here. If a few statements come to mind, write them down and take some time to consider each one.

4. **Read:** Matthew 7:24–25. Why is it important for us to build our mission and our life calling on the foundation of God?

5. What would you do to live out your mission if you had all the money in the world and could do whatever you want to do? Or if you could only do one major thing in the next three years, what would it be? These answers are helpful clues to your life goal(s).

6. What resources fuel your life goals? Are you inspired by *movies, stories, books, people, ideas, spaces,* or *places* to keep living out your vision, goals, or calling?

7. **Read:** 1 Corinthians 7:17–24. What does this passage say about God's calling?

8. What roles do you play in life? Fill in the role map below with your everyday callings.

ROLE MAP FOR LIFE

Individual	Family	Church	Social	Professional
Examples: • faith practices • personal health • activities, adventure	Examples: • spouse • parent • budget manager	Examples: • small group leader • global outreach	Examples: • friends • neighbors • town involvement	Examples: • job responsibilities (list them) • office encourager • outside consulting

9. What roles do you play in your work life? Fill in the role map below. If you need more instruction, read *What's Best Next*, page 183. You may alter the categories based on the work you do.

ROLE MAP FOR WORK

Your Current Title:				
Individual	Team	Leadership	Company	External Industry
List specific roles you fill:	List specific ways you contribute to your team:	List specific ways you lead at work:	List specific roles you play in your company:	List specific roles you play outside your work as they relate to what you do:

10. How do you manage your goals? What kind of season or situation initiates change in your goals?

Take Action: If you are still wrestling with how to *define* your mission, vision, goals, and roles, then create a "Mind Map" to keep working on these definitions. You can create your own or check out these online resources to see which flow works best for you: Mind Manager, Omni Outliner, or use the "Task Manager" feature in OmniFocus or Microsoft Outlook.

CLOSING PRAYER

- Ask God to help you define what matters most as you clarify your mission, vision, goals, and roles.
- If one of these areas seems unclear, ask God to show you or remind you of your ambitions and passions in your everyday life. When you notice these passions and ambitions this week, thank God for his gentle reminders.
- Pray for the areas in your life where you are held back by fear, lack of clarity, or apathy. Ask God to give you the drive and energy to keep moving forward.
- Thank God for providing a gospel-centered method to productivity as a way to help you bring glory to his name. Thank God that you get to be a part of what he is doing in and around the world.

IN BETWEEN SESSIONS

EXERCISE ONE: Your Life Mission

Personal Reflection

Take time in personal reflection to think about the following questions.

➤ Since our life purpose has already been defined by God—*to love God and love others*—then your mission is the individual and unique way you express your life purpose. With that in mind, how would you define—or redefine—your life mission? If you are struggling to answer this question, revisit your answers to question 2 in the *Reflection Questions*.

➤ Matt Perman suggests that we can fail at goals in life and still succeed at our mission, and therefore succeed in our lives. How has this been true for you?

Digging Deeper

Read the following passages and consider how these passages influence your life mission.

Read: Galatians 6:1–10

➤ How does this passage inspire you to create your own life mission for the good of others and the glory of God?

➤ This passage encourages us not to compare ourselves to others. Why is it so tempting to compare our own life mission to the mission of others?

Read: Micah 6:8

➤ In *What's Best Next*, we see a few verses as mission statements from the Bible, including this particular passage. What is the core purpose, and the core principles and beliefs we hear in this verse?

➤ What are the principles and beliefs that drive your life? List a few here.

Personal Action Steps

Consider action steps you can take as a result of what you read today.

➤ Now it's your turn to put all of the pieces together in one place. Follow the prompts provided here to put your life mission statement together. If you need more inspiration, check out the sample on page 163 in *What's Best Next*.

TWO STEPS TO YOUR MISSION STATEMENT

STEP ONE:
Your Core Purpose
(the biblical reason for your existence, in your own words)

_____

_____

_____

Your Guiding Principles
(the general and specific principles you use to guide your life)

1. _____
2. _____
3. _____

Your Core Beliefs
(your identity as a child of God and your destination to glorify God)

_____

_____

_____

STEP TWO:
Mission: Your *Why*

_____

_____

_____

Reflection and Prayer

Spend a few minutes in quiet personal reflection with God. Pray about whatever is on your mind as you consider your life mission and vision. Or use these prayer suggestions as a guide:

- Tell God how you want to live your life with purpose and passion for his glory.
- If you're still searching for words or phrases to describe your *why* and your *what* in life, ask God to show you what your life mission and vision should be or could be.
- Thank God for the unique and individual way he's gifted you to make a difference in the world as you glorify his name.

"God created you and defined your purpose. Your role is to know what that purpose is, embrace it, and state it in a way that captures your own individuality and uniqueness."
—Matt Perman, *What's Best Next*

EXERCISE TWO: Your Life Calling

Personal Reflection

Take time in personal reflection to think about the following questions.

➤ How would you describe your life calling—also known as your *life goals* or your *vision*?

> Remember, your vision is your mission in action—it's the way you live out the most important reason for your existence. *Example: If love is your mission, then providing a safe place for children might be your life goal.*

➤ Why do you want to accomplish these life goals or this vision?

Digging Deeper

Read the following passages and consider how these passages influence your perspective on your life calling.

Read: Romans 15:14–21

➤ What is Paul's vision according to this passage?

➤ How does this inspire you to pursue your vision or life calling?

Read: Matthew 28:18–20

➤ Here Jesus is giving vision to the disciples. What does Jesus ask the disciples to accomplish in his name?

➤ Imagine Jesus standing or sitting with you right now. What vision or life goals do you think Jesus is asking you to accomplish?

Personal Action Steps

Consider action steps you can take as a result of what you read today.

➤ Let's put your mission and vision pieces together. Follow the prompts provided to put your life mission and vision statement side by side. Be specific with your vision or your goals. And if you feel stuck, revisit your answer to question 5 in the *Reflection Questions* section.

PUTTING IT ALL TOGETHER

MISSION: YOUR *WHY*

(Copy your mission statement here from the previous exercise.)

_____

_____

_____

VISION: YOUR *WHAT*

(Also known as your life goals or your calling, these are the aims you want to accomplish in life.)

1. _____

2. _____

3. _____

Reflection and Prayer

Spend a few minutes in quiet personal reflection with God. Pray about whatever is on your mind as you consider your life goals. Or use these prayer suggestions as a guide:

- Dream big and tell God your life goals even if you're scared to write them down or say them out loud because they seem larger than life.
- Ask God to help you live out your vision, even when you fall short or fail trying. Your mission will keep you on track, even if you have to pause and regroup with your goals.
- Thank God for the aims, desires, and passions he's placed on your heart as you live out your calling and pursue your life purpose to glorify God in all you do.

"Thinking big and aiming high for the glory of God puts us in the realm of our life calling or vision."
—Matt Perman, *What's Best Next*

EXERCISE THREE: Your Roles and Goals

Personal Reflection

Take time in personal reflection to think about the following questions.

➤ Reflect on the roles you listed in the section on *Reflection Questions.* What
stands out to you as you reflect on your roles? Are there any roles you would
add or combine?

➤ How do you accomplish your life goals through the roles you play? *Example:
William Wilberforce accomplished his life goal of ending the slave trade in Britain by
playing a role in the British parliament.*

Digging Deeper

*Read the following passages and consider how these passages influence your perspective on your
roles and goals.*

Read: Proverbs 16:1–9

➤ What stands out to you in this passage as it relates to pursuing your goals?

➤ Has there ever been a time when you put a lot of planning into your goals, only for God to change the plans? What happened?

Read: Philippians 3:12–21

➤ What does this passage say about goals?

➤ How does Paul's perspective on goals inspire you as you pursue your goals?

Personal Action Steps

Consider action steps you can take as a result of what you read today.

➤ List your top three primary roles in life and the main goal you have for each one of those roles. These can be goals related to the specific role, or general goals that apply to all three roles.

1. _____

2. _____

3. _____

Reflection and Prayer

Spend a few minutes in quiet personal reflection with God. Pray about whatever is on your mind as you consider the roles you play in life and the goals you use to make the most of those roles. Or use these prayer suggestions as a guide:

- Tell God how much you want to embrace the roles you've been given and apply your life goal to each area of these roles.
- Ask God to show you if there are roles and goals you have been neglecting and need to give more attention to. Or if there are roles and goals you need to let go of in order to better serve other people or areas of your life.
- Thank God for giving you opportunities to go out of your way to do good for the sake of others as you live out your life goal(s) in each of your roles.

"Your roles are all callings from God and thus avenues of worship. You can serve him just as fully in the 'secular' areas of your life as you can in the spiritual areas."
—Matt Perman

EXPLORING ADDITIONAL RESOURCES

Take some time to explore the additional resources recommended in *What's Best Next* session 3:

Rick Warren, "Living with Purpose," chapter 40 of *The Purpose Driven Life*
Stephen Covey, "Habit 2, Begin with the End in Mind," in *The Seven Habits of Highly Effective People*
John Piper, *Don't Waste Your Life*. See specifically the first three chapters.
Keith Ferrazzi, "What's Your Mission?" chapter 3 in *Never Eat Alone*
David Martyn Lloyd-Jones, *Studies in the Sermon on the Mount*
The Resolutions of Jonathan Edwards
David Platt, *Radical*
Francis Chan, *Crazy Love*
John Bunyan, *Pilgrim's Progress*
Stephen Nichols, *Heaven on Earth: Capturing Jonathan Edwards's Vision of Living in Between*
Os Guinness, *The Call: Finding and Fulfilling the Central Purpose of Your Life*
Gene Veith, *God at Work*
Stephen Covey, "The Balance of Roles," chapter 6 in *First Things First*
Andy Stanley, *When Work and Family Collide: Keeping Your Job from Cheating Your Family*

PREPARATION FOR NEXT SESSION

As you reflect on what God is teaching you through this session, read or review part 3: chapters 11–13 of *What's Best Next* by Matt Perman. Also in preparation for your next session, you will want to read part 4: chapters 14–15.

NOTES

ARCHITECT

Create a Flexible Structure

Structured time spent executing ideas is a best practice of admired creative leaders across industries. It is the only way to keep up with the continuous stream of action steps and allocate sufficient time for deep thought.

—Scott Belsky

INTRODUCTION

Creating a Flexible Structure

I'm a list maker. Always have been, always will be. But I'll be the first to admit that there was a season when my lists did more harm than good. I had so many lists that my massive inventory of action items left me with little room in which to do them. What was supposed to relieve my stress—creating lists—was creating even more stress for me. It was like a tsunami of activity that I could never rise above to catch my breath. That's when I realized that something needed to change. It was no longer enough just to have a giant catalog of all of the tasks I needed to accomplish. I needed to find a rhythm, framework, or routine for accomplishing the never-ending lists. And the lightbulb moment for me happened when I realized that my action lists had to be connected to my schedule in some way.

It's easy to think that our tasks and to-dos should govern our schedule, when in fact it's the exact opposite. A basic, daily routine—informed by your mission and roles—is the framework that will enable you to actually get things done on your lists. Lists are essential to support our routine, rather than drive our daily actions. And a basic routine makes our actions more tangible and forces us to stop and ask whether or not we can, and *should*, fit everything on our list into our schedule. Having a basic routine allows us to make time for the roles and responsibilities that are most important to us, as well as gives us the ability to focus and be creative. Good intentions are most often not good enough.

The best routines are also the most flexible routines. This is what allows spontaneity, and therefore, innovation. The point of a basic routine is to keep spontaneous interaction—meetings, conversations, ideas—from getting crowded out by a sense that you always need to be plugging away on your project list. A flexible framework enables innovation.

The key to the second step—the Architect step—of Gospel-Driven Productivity in the acronym DARE is to create a basic structure for your life. This means identifying the most important responsibilities and activities from your roles and placing them into a flexible framework for your week so that it becomes a natural habit for you to get things done during specific periods of time. My hope for you this session is to get to the place where you can "come up for air" from your project lists and begin to think creatively not just about the work you do but also about how you do it. By the end of this session, you will know how to set up your work week, put into action your consistent routines and your "special case" routines, and still have time to be creative. And you will be amazed at the flexibility you have in your schedule when the right routines are in place.

THINK ABOUT IT

➤ What does it look like for you to prep for your work week?

-or-

➤ What kind of rhythms or routines seem to work best for your approach to work?

VIDEO TEACHING NOTES

Setting Up Your Week

How do lists and the schedule connect?

People work best from routines, not lists *(influenced by the life of George Washington).*

Your framework: a routine governed by mission and roles

Setting up your week:

- Set up a prototype week—time map (your weekly schedule).

- Specify a theme for each day.

Benefits of setting up your week:

- Creating activity zones helps efficiency by keeping related tasks together.

- Every task will have a general time slot.

"Instead of feeling that you have to act on every request the minute it crosses your path, you can glance at your Time Map, determine when you have time for this unexpected task, and either schedule it or skip it."
—Julie Morgenstern, *Time Management from the Inside Out*

Creating the Right Routines

The Six Core Routines:

1. Get up early (or stay up late).

2. Daily workflow

> **For Focused, Uninterrupted Work:**
>
> Plan your day.
> Execute your workflow.
> Do your daily main activity.
> Do next actions or major project work.

- Processing new input is important in your daily workflow.

"Knowledge workers spend about 60 minutes per day to process new information."
—David Allen

- Take time to process new information and have a way to do that.

3. Weekly workflow: home tasks—*the structure for your whole life*

4. Prayer and Scripture

5. Reading and development

   • Read Tim Sanders's chapter on "Knowledge" in *Love Is the Killer App.*

   • Keep a reading list.

   • Write in your books.

> **"Marking up a book is not an act of mutilation but of love."**
> **—Mortimer Adler, "How to Mark a Book"**

   • Other ways for learning and growth

6. Rest

REFLECTION QUESTIONS

1. How would you describe your basic routine?

2. Have you ever felt overwhelmed by your to-do list? What happens when you feel this way?

3. Up until this point, would you say you are more of a list person, a schedule person, or both? How so?

4. How does the teaching in this session influence your perception of lists, schedules, and routines?

5. What is most challenging for you when it comes to maintaining your schedule and routine?

6. What does it look like for you to maintain space for creative thinking? What kind of creativity are you drawn to in that space: *writing, painting, drawing, brainstorming, designing, exploring, creating something with your hands or your mind, etc.?*

7. **Read:** Daniel 6. What stands out to you about Daniel's routine? How does God honor Daniel's commitment to his routine and to God?

8. Out of the six core routines mentioned in this teaching session, which one comes most easily to you? Which one is the hardest?

9. **Read:** Luke 21:37–38. What does this passage tell us about Jesus' routine?

10. How did Jesus maintain his mission by practicing this routine? Can you think of examples of how Jesus exercised flexibility in his structured routine? Consider ways you maintain your mission by developing your own flexible routine.

	Sunday	Monday	Tuesday
Goal:	Family/Rest/Spiritual	Accomplish week/meetings	
6:00 AM			
6:30 AM			
7:00 AM		Prayer	Prayer
7:30 AM	Prayer	Breakfast/commute	Breakfast/commute
8:00 AM		Daily Workflow	Daily Workflow
8:30 AM			
9:00 AM		Projects	Projects
9:30 AM			
10:00 AM	Church/SS		
10:30 AM			
11:00 AM			
11:30 AM		Lunch/Free	Lunch/Free
12:00 PM			
12:30 PM		Meetings/Other	Meetings/Other
1:00 PM	People		
1:30 PM			
2:00 PM			
2:30 PM			
3:00 PM			
3:30 PM			
4:00 PM	Free	*Afternoon workflow*	*Afternoon workflow*
4:30 PM			
5:00 PM		Exercise	Exercise
5:30 PM			
6:00 PM	Family	Family: *Play with kids/homework*	Family *Play with kids/ homework*
6:30 PM			
7:00 PM			
7:30 PM			
8:00 PM	*Bedtimes*		*Bedtimes*
8:30 PM		Blog	
9:00 PM			
9:30 PM	Free		Free
10:00 PM			
10:30 PM			
11:00 PM			
11:30 PM	Sleep	Sleep	Sleep
12:00 AM			

Wednesday	Thursday	Friday	Saturday	Goal:
Accomplish week/meetings		Projects/development	Family	
				6:00 AM
				6:30 AM
Prayer	Prayer	Prayer		7:00 AM
Breakfast/commute	Breakfast/commute			7:30 AM
Daily Workflow	Daily Workflow	Daily Workflow Reading Pile	Weekly Workflow	8:00 AM
				8:30 AM
Projects	Projects	Projects/Learning		9:00 AM
				9:30 AM
			Exercise	10:00 AM
				10:30 AM
				11:00 AM
Lunch/Free	Lunch/Free			11:30 AM
				12:00 PM
Meetings/Other	Meetings/Other		Family Activity	12:30 PM
				1:00 PM
				1:30 PM
				2:00 PM
				2:30 PM
				3:00 PM
				3:30 PM
Afternoon workflow	*Afternoon workflow*		Free	4:00 PM
				4:30 PM
Exercise	Exercise	Free		5:00 PM
				5:30 PM
Family *Play with kids/ homework*	Family *Play with kids/ homework*		Family Night	6:00 PM
				6:30 PM
				7:00 PM
				7:30 PM
Bedtimes	*Bedtimes*	People		8:00 PM
			Bedtimes	8:30 PM
Free	Free		Free	9:00 PM
				9:30 PM
				10:00 PM
				10:30 PM
Sleep	Sleep	Sleep	Sleep	11:00 PM
				11:30 PM
				12:00 AM

Take Action: Create a Time Map for your week, like the one on pages 200–201 in *What's Best Next*. How would you arrange, or rearrange, your schedule to create a healthy routine for deciding what's best next and getting things done? What do you need to move to create the right routines in your life?

> *"The goal is to find routines that help you turn your mission statement, your life goals, and your weekly schedules into practices that reflect your priorities."*
> —Matt Perman, *What's Best Next*

CLOSING PRAYER

- Ask God to help you find a rhythm and routine that works best for you, so that you can work best for God.
- Ask God to show you where to build in flexibility and maintain creativity in your schedule, as this is necessary to loving and serving others to the best of our abilities.
- Pray for the areas in your life that might be hurdles to developing healthy schedules and routines. Reflect on what those hurdles might be: *fear, perfection, apathy, indifference, etc.*
- Thank God for providing a gospel-centered approach to productivity and its influence on the way you spend your time at work, with your family, in the community, and at church. And thank God for the freedom to be the architect of your own flexible structure.

IN BETWEEN SESSIONS

EXERCISE ONE: How to Set Up Your Week

Personal Reflection

Take time in personal reflection to think about the following questions.

➤ How does it make you feel or what does it make you think to consider giving up your to-do lists in order to create a more flexible routine?

➤ Revisit your Time Map from the reflection questions. If you didn't get to fill it out, do so now. Reflect on your daily *and* weekly routines. What do you notice about your schedule? What is going well, and what immediate changes do you need to make regarding how you spend your time?

Digging Deeper

Read the following passages and consider how these passages influence the way you schedule your time.

Read: Hebrews 10:19–25

➤ What habits do you notice in this passage?

➤ What does it look like for you to prioritize time with your friends and your community? Is this time already included in your schedule? If not, where can you add it into your weekly routine?

Read: 2 Timothy 1:7

➤ What does the Spirit of God give to us, according to this verse?

➤ Several translations of the Bible use the words *self-control* or *self-discipline*. How have you exercised self-control or self-discipline as it relates to your daily and weekly routines?

Personal Action Steps

Consider action steps you can take as a result of what you read today.

➤ Reflect on the four core tasks of your daily workflow and add specific examples and time frames to these tasks. Then put them into practice this week and see what happens.

1. **Plan your day:** Review appointments, tasks, and any last-minute activities.
   _____

   Approximate time to complete: _____

2. **Execute your workflow:** Respond to email and voice mail, and check notes —respond to all your sources of input. _____
   _____

   Approximate time to complete: _____

3. **Do your main daily activity:** leading, writing, teaching, parenting, etc.
   _____

   Approximate time to complete: _____

4. **Do some next actions or major project work:** _____
   _____

   Approximate time to complete: _____

Now put these tasks into action!

Reflection and Prayer

Spend a few minutes in quiet personal reflection with God. Pray about whatever is on your mind as you consider your daily and weekly routines. Or use these prayer suggestions as a guide:

- Tell God how you want to live your life to be free for what he wants you to do, even if this means scheduling your time more than you're used to and saying no to the things that don't fit into your schedule.
- If you're still struggling with how to fit everything into your schedule, ask God to show you where you need more structure and where you need more flexibility.
- Thank God for giving you the gifts and abilities to do the work that you do, and for the opportunities you have to be insanely good at something.

"You tame time through a routine—knowing what's around the corner, and knowing how much time you have to do it. Not all of your time is routine, but enough needs to be to create a framework."
—Bradley Blakeman in an interview with Matt Perman, *What's Best Next*

EXERCISE TWO: Weaving in Your Routines

Personal Reflection

Take time in personal reflection to think about the following questions.

➤ Do you have the opportunity to do what you do best every day? If not, is there something you want to get good at—something that makes a difference for you and others and your organization?

➤ What changes can you make to your main daily activity in order to incorporate more of the activity that you do best?

Digging Deeper

Read the following passages and consider how these passages influence your perspective on creating the right routines.

Read: Exodus 18:17–27

➤ What made Moses decide to adjust his routine?

➤ How did Moses pursue the *right* routine?

Read: Judges 4:4–5

➤ What was Deborah's work routine?

➤ Why do you think this was the right routine for Deborah? If you have access to a study Bible or an online version, take a few minutes to understand the context of Deborah's time and place to see why this was the right routine for her.

Personal Action Steps

Consider action steps you can take as a result of what you read today.

➤ Revisit the six core routines in chapter 15 of *What's Best Next*, and rate yourself on a scale of 1–10, 1 being "Needs help!" and 10 being "Doing amazing!"

1. Get up early (or stay up late):
2. Daily workflow:
3. Weekly workflow:
4. Prayer and Scripture:
5. Reading and development:
6. Rest:

➤ Pick one of the routines where you need the most work. What's one step you can take today to improve this routine in your life? _____

_____

Reflection and Prayer

Spend a few minutes in quiet personal reflection with God. Pray about whatever is on your mind as you consider the right routines for your life. Or use these prayer suggestions as a guide:

- Ask God to help you determine the *right* routines for your life.
- Ask God to help you remember that the *right* routines allow you to live out your mission and life goals so that your practices reflect your priorities, and so that you can bring glory to God's name in the big and small things in life.
- Thank God for the routine of rest and other routines—like exercise, family night, dinner out with friends—that fill your bucket instead of causing you to feel tired and overwhelmed.

"Routines shouldn't invent new work for you. They should capture the work you already do and put it into a framework that lets you do it more efficiently."
—Matt Perman, *What's Best Next*

EXERCISE THREE: Making Room for Creativity

Personal Reflection

Take time in personal reflection to think about the following questions.

➤ When you are consistent with a daily schedule and the right kind of routine for you, you actually have more space for creativity and innovation. From your perspective, what does it mean to be creative? Or what does it look like for you to practice creativity?

➤ How has the space for creativity in your life allowed you to be innovative at work, at home, or in one of your many roles?

Digging Deeper

Read the following passages and consider how these passages influence your perspective on your creativity and innovation.

Read: Genesis 1:26–27

➤ If you truly believe this passage, then where does your creativity come from?

➤ How does thinking about God's creativity and innovation in the creation of the world influence your own creativity and innovation?

Read: Romans 12:2

➤ What do you think Paul means in this passage when he says, "Be transformed by the renewing of your mind"?

➤ How does renewing your mind foster creativity and innovation when it comes to your relationship with God?

Personal Action Steps

Consider action steps you can take as a result of what you read today.

➤ List three activities that spark creativity for you, or creative activities you've wanted to try. Do at least one of them this week.

_____

_____

_____

Reflection and Prayer

Spend a few minutes in quiet personal reflection with God. Pray about whatever is on your mind as you consider creativity and innovation. Or use these prayer suggestions as a guide:

- Tell God how much you want to have space for creativity and innovation in your everyday life. Maybe you don't consider yourself creative; if so, ask God to help reframe your perspective on creativity.
- Ask God to remind you of moments when you were at your creative and innovative best in the past as inspiration for your present.
- Thank God for making you in his image—his creative and innovative image. Spend a few moments of silence reflecting on your gratitude.

> "Make a careful exploration of who you are and the work you have been given, and then sink yourself into that. Don't be impressed with yourself. Don't compare yourself with others. Each of you must take responsibility for doing the creative best you can with your own life."
> —Galatians 6:4–5, The Message

EXPLORING ADDITIONAL RESOURCES

Take some time to explore the additional resources recommended in *What's Best Next* session 4:

Julia Cameron, *The Artist's Way*
Erwin McManus, *The Artisan Soul*
Jordan Raynor, *Called to Create*

PREPARATION FOR NEXT SESSION

As you reflect on what God is teaching you through this session, read or review part 4: chapters 14–15 of *What's Best Next* by Matt Perman. Also in preparation for your next session, you will want to read part 5: chapters 16–18.

NOTES

_____

_____

_____

_____

_____

_____

_____

_____

_____

_____

_____

_____

_____

_____

_____

_____

_____

_____

REDUCE

Free Up Your Time for What's Most Important

Learning how to cope with not getting everything done
is just as important as getting more done.
—Stuart Levine, *Cut to the Chase*

INTRODUCTION

When Things Fall Apart

I'm guessing most of us have been there. That moment when we forgot to pick up a kid from practice, or double-booked appointments, or neglected to add something to our calendar and missed an important conversation or meeting. We often race from one engagement to the next, trying to squeeze in as much as possible but not really showing up fully present to anything because we're so preoccupied by showing up late and leaving early. We try to be a good friend or teammate to everyone, and in doing so, end up not really being a good friend or teammate to anyone because we've spread ourselves too thin relationally. Or we get so busy doing things *for* God that we miss out on time *with* God. We add more balls and more tasks to the daily juggle of our lives only to realize that we could barely handle juggling three balls, let alone ten balls. It's easy to get into this kind of mess with our schedules and tasks, but how do we get out of it? That's what this session is all about: *reducing* the amount of tasks in our lives so we have the freedom to focus on what's most important.

For example, have you ever considered why traffic slows down inexplicably during rush hour? If you've ever driven through a major city like Los Angeles, Chicago, New York, or Philadelphia at five p.m. on a weekday, then you know what I mean. However, unless there's some kind of accident or major highway construction, there's no reason traffic should be going that slow. The reason it does go slow is because someone slightly hit their brakes four miles ahead. Under normal circumstances, slightly tapping the brakes would have no effect on the flow of traffic. But during rush hour, when the highway capacity is past 90 percent, small disturbances have a huge effect. This is why traffic slows to a crawl. The same thing happens at airports, sports stadiums, and numerous places around the world. Whenever systems reach or exceed 90 percent capacity, efficiency drops *dramatically*, and small disturbances have a huge effect. The same thing happens in our work lives too. When you are working on a lot of things at the same time, those tasks will often "bump into" one another and cause the same effect. That's why our projects or assignments sit in a queue for much longer than necessary. Reaching max capacity has a cascading effect in our lives.

This brings us to the focus of this session. In order to get more projects done, you need to reduce the number of projects you are working on at once. Believe it or not, the max capacity for individuals and organizations is 75 percent, compared to 90 percent in the transportation infrastructure. This means we have to take this topic seriously if we want to maximize the way we spend our time getting the most important things done.

The third step in Gospel-Driven Productivity is *reduce*. This means to free up your time for what's most important. You do this by reducing the amount of tasks you attempt to accomplish every day, or every week, so you can focus on what's most important and actually get things done. My hope for you this session is to get to the place where your tasks are manageable and you no longer feel like you're constantly dropping the balls you are juggling. By the end of this session, you will understand why doing less actually enables you to do more, how delegating matters when it comes to freeing up your time, and how to handle the time killers in your life.

THINK ABOUT IT

➤ What are the biggest time killers in your personal and professional life?

-or-

➤ How do you know when you are juggling too much? What are the signs or symptoms?

VIDEO TEACHING NOTES

The Problem with Full System Utilization

Projects and chaos theory:

The Ringing Effect: When capacity exceeds 90 percent, efficiency drops massively.

The relationship between chaos theory and managing your projects:

> *"Since 'all white-collar work is essentially project oriented,' it follows that all knowledge workers 'are faced with the likely occurrence of chaos within their daily activities.'"*
> —Robert Munson, *Professor*

The way to get better at work: reduce the number of projects you are working on at once.

The Ringing Effect for organizations and individuals begins at 75 percent capacity.

The Art of Making Time: *Delegation*

David Allen's *Getting Things Done (GTD)*

Tim Challies's *The Next Story: Life and Faith after the Digital Explosion*

Peter Drucker's *The Effective Executive*

Four main ways to reduce:

1. Delegate

2. Eliminate

3. Automate

4. Defer

Delegation:

- builds up the other person

- builds up the capacity of the organization

Stewardship delegation versus gopher delegation:

- Gopher delegation—responsibility lies with you.

- Stewardship delegation—true responsibility is handed over to them.

Five Components of Effective Stewardship Delegation, from *First Things First:*

1. **Desired Results:** *the what*

2. **Guidelines:** *the parameters*

3. **Resources:** *what's available to help with the task*

4. **Accountability:** *the framework that provides accountability and rewards results*

5. **Consequences:** *consistent meetings to assess where you're at*

The role of a manager in stewardship delegation:

- The manager should manage from values.

- The manager is a source of help, not a boss.

The learning curve of delegation: the higher up-front time investment

Overcoming Procrastination and Interruptions:
Harnessing the Time Killers

Two of the biggest time killers are *procrastination* and *interruptions*.

Procrastination:

The best way to overcome procrastination is to: Love what you do.

Three chief components of motivation from Dan Pink's book *Drive: The Surprising Truth about What Motivates Us*

1. **Autonomy:** *Do you have the freedom to do these tasks in your own way?*

2. **Mastery:** *Are the tasks too hard or too easy?*

3. **Purpose:** *Do you believe in the purpose of your tasks?*

Intrinsic motivation: *To be pulled toward motivation rather than pushed toward motivation*

Three main tactics of procrastination:

1. We are not ready.

2. The task is overwhelming.

3. Procrastinate positively: Do nothing.

Interruptions:

> *"I argue that when people are switching contexts every ten and a half minutes they can't possibly be thinking deeply. There's no way people can achieve flow. When I write a research article, it takes me a couple of hours before I can even begin to think creatively. If I was switching every ten and a half minutes, there's just no way I'd be able to think deeply about what I'm doing. This is really bad for innovation. When you're on the treadmill like this, it's just not possible to achieve flow."*
> —Gloria Mark quoted in Kermit Pattison, "Worker
> Interrupted: The Cost of Task Switching," *Fast Company*

Strategies for harnessing interruptions:

1. Have an uninterrupted zone for work at the beginning of your day.

2. Embrace interruptions as opportunities to do good for others.

> *"The great thing, if one can, is to stop regarding all the unpleasant things as interruptions of one's 'own,' or 'real' life. The truth is of course that what one calls the interruptions are precisely one's real life—the life God is sending one day by day; what one calls one's 'real life' is a phantom of one's own imagination. This at least is what I see at moments of insight; but it's hard to remember it all the time."*
> —C. S. Lewis, letter to Arthur Greeves, December
> 29, 1943, in *The Quotable Lewis*

"Successful executives turn one key time management rule upside down: rather than closing the door on interruptions, they extract genuine value from them."
—Stephanie Winston, *Organized for Success*

REFLECTION QUESTIONS

1. What stood out to you about the teaching? How can you identify with Matt Perman's own examples?

2. Have you ever reached max capacity with your tasks and projects? Briefly describe the situation or circumstances.

3. What factors contributed to you reaching max capacity? *For example: work requirements, expectations of others, people-pleasing, personal standards, your interpretation of what it means to be a "good" Christian?*

4. Which one of the four main ways to reduce are you already doing well— *delegate, eliminate, automate, defer*? Give brief examples. And which do you need to work on?

5. **Read:** Nehemiah 3. Nehemiah gives us a healthy example of what it looks like to delegate as he rebuilds the walls of Jerusalem. How many names are mentioned here under Nehemiah's delegation? And what kinds of work are they doing?

6. Now it's your turn. How many people are you delegating to right now? And what kinds of things are you delegating?

7. Consider the time killers you mentioned earlier. Which time killers have the most impact on the amount of work you are able to accomplish?

8. Which time killers can you eliminate? Which time killers do you think would actually help if they were harnessed for good?

9. **Read:** Luke 8:43–48. Who interrupted Jesus and why? How did Jesus respond?

10. How do you respond to interruptions? Where does this response come from? *More on this in the In Between Session Exercise Three.*

Take Action: Do one thing today to *delegate, eliminate, automate,* or *defer.* Now make it your goal to do one thing from one of these ways every day this week. Mark this page and keep track of whatever you decide to delegate, eliminate, automate, or defer, and take note of how it impacts your overall schedule.

DAY 1: Action: _____

Impact: _____

DAY 2: Action: _____

Impact: _____

DAY 3: Action: _____

Impact: _____

DAY 4: Action: _____

Impact: _____

DAY 5: Action: _____

Impact: _____

> *"Resolved, never to lose one moment of time; but improve*
> *it the most profitable way I possibly can."*
> —Jonathan Edwards, *Resolution 5*

CLOSING PRAYER

- Ask God to help you this week by showing you where you're juggling too much, and what needs to be reduced in your life.
- Ask God to show you what needs to be *delegated, eliminated, automated,* and *deferred.*
- Pray for the opportunities to invite other people into your projects and tasks so you can work together according to your strengths and abilities, and in doing so, get more done and bring glory to God *together.*
- Thank God for the interruptions he brings your way, and thank God for what he is teaching you through those interruptions.

IN BETWEEN SESSIONS

EXERCISE ONE: Do Less to Do More

Personal Reflection

Take time in personal reflection to think about the following questions.

➤ How does running at max capacity for a while start to affect you physically, emotionally, mentally, relationally, spiritually, and so on? And how does it affect the people around you?

➤ What is your greatest challenge to doing less so you can do more?

Digging Deeper

Read the following passages and consider how these passages influence the way you consider your capacity.

Read: Colossians 4:2–6

➤ What do you think Paul means when he says, "Make the most of every opportunity"?

➤ What keeps you from making the most of every opportunity right now?

Read: 2 Corinthians 4:16–18

➤ We often get so focused on the "seen" parts of our lives that we forget the "unseen"—the parts where we have the most opportunity to bring glory to God. Things like *showing love and grace to a difficult coworker when collaborating on a project, helping your child develop empathy by including them as you make a meal for a new neighbor, studying with a new classmate so they feel connected and known on campus . . .* you get the idea. What are a few things you could do this week to focus on tasks like these that bring glory to God in the "unseen" parts of your life?

➤ What do you need to cut out this week in order to shift your focus?

Personal Action Steps

Consider action steps you can take as a result of what you read today.

➤ Reflect on the "unseen" tasks you mentioned above. Pick one task, possibly an act of service, you could do *with* someone else *for* someone else. And then do it.

Unseen Task: _____

I will partner with _____ to accomplish this task.

Date to be accomplished: _____

Tasks I will cut out in order to do this act of service: _____

Reflection and Prayer

Spend a few minutes in quiet personal reflection with God. Pray about whatever is on your mind as you consider the idea of doing less so you can do more. Or use these prayer suggestions as a guide:

- Tell God how you want to do less so you can do more for him, but if this is a struggle for you, explain why this is a struggle.
- Ask God to show you what to focus on more and what to focus on less in order to be more productive in your life and bring more glory to him.
- Thank God for the limits he's given you and given to all of us as humans. Because of these limits, we are more aware of our need for God and our need for others. Express your gratitude to God for the specific people who help you accomplish your tasks and projects in this season.

_____

_____

_____

_____

_____

_____

_____

_____

_____

_____

_____

_____

> *"The first step in learning to reduce is rejecting the "solo mentality"—the notion that productivity is merely an individual matter. With this mentality, you end up isolating yourself, which is the opposite of what God wants for us. God designed the world so that there will always be more things for us to do than we are able to do. This isn't just so we learn to prioritize; it's so that we learn to depend on one another."*
> —Matt Perman, *What's Best Next*

EXERCISE TWO: How to Free Up Your Time

Personal Reflection

Take time in personal reflection to think about the following questions.

➤ How are you *doing less in order to do more* this week by putting these ways into practice? Give specific examples.

• Delegating:

• Automating:

• Eliminating:

• Deferring:

➤ How are you inviting others into your projects, tasks, and responsibilities, and in doing so, building them up? Name a few specific people who are impacted by your healthier choices this week.

Digging Deeper

Read the following passages and consider how these passages influence the way you spend your time.

Read: 1 Timothy 4:11–16

➤ What do you notice about the way Paul delegates his mission to Timothy? How does Paul build Timothy up with encouragement and challenges?

➤ Do you have a Paul or Timothy in your life? If so, how does that relationship make you better at what you do?

Read: Matthew 28:16–20

➤ What did Jesus delegate? And to whom did he delegate?

➤ Why was this significant in the history of the early church? Why is this significant to us today?

Personal Action Steps

Consider action steps you can take as a result of what you read today.

Delegation Styles

- Gopher delegation: when you hand people specific tasks as the need arises, and then you supervise them closely with how they accomplish those tasks.
- Stewardship delegation: when you delegate tasks and allow the individual to determine their own methods for accomplishing the tasks.

➤ Review these delegation styles. Think about a specific relationship or situation in which you need to switch from *gopher*-style delegation to *stewardship*-style delegation. It can be a situation at work, at home, in the classroom, or with volunteers from church, and so on. Take action by making that switch today and communicating that switch with the individuals involved in the project. Also, be sure to fill out the **Take Action** section of *Reflection Questions*.

Reflection and Prayer

Spend a few minutes in quiet personal reflection with God. Pray about whatever is on your mind as you consider ways to free up your time. Or use these prayer suggestions as a guide:

- Ask God to help you specifically with the four practices that allow you to free up your time: *delegating, eliminating, automating,* and *deferring.*
- Ask God to help you see the bigger picture as you put these practices in place. The bigger picture may include changing the trajectory of someone else's life by delegating, or freeing up more of your time to be with your family, and in all of these things, bringing ultimate glory to God.
- Thank God for giving you the freedom and opportunity to wrestle with your time and your tasks as you figure out how to creatively make the most of your time. What a gift!

"The aim [of good stewardship and delegation] is not just to get things done, but to develop the people in the process."
—Matt Perman, *What's Best Next*

EXERCISE THREE: Harness the Time Killers

Personal Reflection

Take time in personal reflection to think about the following questions.

➤ Which time killers are most frustrating to you? Which ones are in your control, and which ones are out of your control?

The Most Common Time Killers

1. Multitasking (switch tasking, background tasking, and rapid refocusing)
2. Procrastination
3. Interruptions
4. Social networking

➤ If interruptions are challenging for you, consider the examples Matt Perman shared about creating "interruptible" time and space. This is one of several ways you can harness a time killer for good. When is the optimal time and where is your optimal space to focus and not be interrupted? Where is the space and when is the time when it's *acceptable* to be interrupted?

➤ Map it out now so you can follow through tomorrow. Also pay attention to how much you interrupt yourself during your focused work. *For example: social media, checking your phone, etc.*

Digging Deeper

Read the following passages and consider how these passages describe the various ways we can respond to time killers.

Read: Mark 1:35–38

➤ There are numerous examples of moments when Jesus gets interrupted throughout the New Testament. This one stands out because Jesus gets interrupted during what most might consider an "inopportune" time. What was Jesus doing at the moment he was interrupted and how did he respond?

Read: Jonah 1

➤ What happened as a result of Jonah's procrastination in going to Nineveh?

➤ Have you ever had to learn the hard way, like Jonah, about deferring or procrastinating on a big task? Or have you watched someone else go through this? Either way, what lessons did you learn?

Personal Action Steps

Consider action steps you can take as a result of what you read today.

➤ List one way you can harness each time killer for good, based on what you learned in this session, and what you have read from chapter 18 in *What's Best Next*:

Multitasking: _____

Procrastination: _____

Interruptions: _____

Social networking: _____

Reflection and Prayer

Spend a few minutes in quiet personal reflection with God. Pray about whatever is on your mind as you consider harnessing your time killers for good. Or use these prayer suggestions as a guide:

- Tell God where you are most frustrated or confused with these time killers.
- Ask God to give you clarity about harnessing these time killers for good and knowing when to eliminate a time killer.
- Thank God for the gift of being interrupted and the way God uses these interruptions to speak to you or show you something he wants you to see.

_____

_____

_____

_____

_____

_____

_____

_____

_____

_____

_____

_____

_____

_____

_____

_____

"We need to both carve out time for focused work and then also weave into our days the flexibility to be freely available so that we can recognize interruptions as opportunities for productive interactions. There is a both/and here: minimize interruptions. And realize that there is a way to make use of interruptions for maximum effectiveness."
—Matt Perman, *What's Best Next*

EXPLORING ADDITIONAL RESOURCES

Take some time to explore the additional resources recommended in *What's Best Next* session 5:

Timothy Ferriss, *The Four-Hour Workweek*

Marcus Buckingham, *The One Thing You Need to Know*

Michael Hyatt, www.michaelhyatt.com/should-you-consider-hiring-a-virtual
-assistant.html

Sharon Begley, "The Science of Making Decisions" *Newsweek* (February 27, 2011),
http://www.newsweek.com/science-making-decisions-68627

PREPARATION FOR NEXT SESSION

As you reflect on what God is teaching you through this session, read or review part 5: chapters 16–18 of *What's Best Next* by Matt Perman. Also, in preparation for your next session, you will want to read part 6: chapters 19–22.

NOTES

EXECUTE

Do What's Most Important

Effective executives do first things first and they do one thing at a time.
—Peter Drucker, *The Effective Executive*

INTRODUCTION

Do What's Most Important

This session is all about doing what's most important. This is often called *executing*. Up until now, we've talked about *identifying* what's most important, but this is where we turn the corner and take action. Besides, what good does talking and planning do if we never get our ideas off the ground?

Sometimes taking action requires a little self-awareness. We need to ask ourselves if we are more comfortable *identifying* action steps or *taking* action steps. If you're more comfortable with *thinking* rather than with *doing,* consider why. Have you had a bad past experience with taking action on a big project? Do you get caught up in trying to reach perfection, paralyzed to take action until everything seems just right? Are you constantly falling short of your own ideals or the expectations of others, and therefore, a bit scared to move into motion? Or are you hesitant to take action because you're out of your league in your role and do not quite understand the task at hand? There could be other reasons, even memories from adolescent years that still influence the way you make decisions and take action in your adult life. Or the hurdle to executing could simply be that you haven't discovered the *best* way to take action until now. Either way, moving forward for any one of us can only happen when we are willing to address what it is that has kept us from taking action up until this point.

It's also important to note that not everything that comes at us in a typical work week is worth doing, but some things are, and we can't do them all at once. That's why we need a system for executing; otherwise we will suffocate ourselves, or even worse, risk burnout. We need to learn how to execute well in order to do what's best next.

The fourth and final step in Gospel-Driven Productivity is *execute*. This means living out our priorities every moment of every day. And one of the major tools for this phase is the classic to-do list. Yes, we're back to the to-do list, but this time we will learn to maximize the to-do list in order to support our priorities. My hope for you this session is that you learn how to plan in advance for a productive work week, while simultaneously and comfortably navigating your day in the moment. By the end of this session, you will know how to effectively plan each week, organize new input that comes at you every day, and execute your priorities by taking purposeful action.

THINK ABOUT IT

➤ What's more comfortable for you—thinking about a plan or taking action on a plan? Why?

-or-

➤ What is your biggest hurdle to executing a project?

VIDEO TEACHING NOTES

Three-Step Process to Executing: POD

1. **Plan:** *weekly planning*

2. **Organize:** *managing your workflow*

3. **Do:** *making things happen*

Weekly Planning

Create a basic plan for your week: *Determine what is important and organize around it.*

But the big rocks in first.

Three Steps for a Weekly Review:

1. Pray and review the higher altitudes (mission and vision).
2. Define your priorities for the week.
3. Organize your priorities in a way that makes them easy to do.

Weekly planning: *the breakdown*

1. Prayer and review:

   • Pray for your week.

"Commit your work to the Lord, and your plans will be established."
—Proverbs 16:3 ESV

   • Review your mission and vision.

2. Define your priorities for the week:

   • Reflect—ask yourself, *"What do I need to do this week?"* and *"What would I like to do this week?"*

   • Review your roles and goals—*adapt the "reflect" questions according to your roles and goals.*

   • Review your project and action lists—*create a routine to make this a regular practice; write down big steps you need to take that week.*

   • Review your calendar—*look at upcoming events you need to prepare for and follow up with what you missed last week.*

   • Get creative about doing good—*ask yourself these three questions:*

      1. What actions can I take against injustice this week?

> **"Learn to do good; seek justice, correct oppression; bring justice to the fatherless, plead the widow's cause."**
> **—Isaiah 1:17 ESV**

      2. What can I do proactively for the good of my family, neighbors, coworkers, and community?

3. What action can I take in the fight against large global problems?

- Making a routine of giving deliberate thought will have massive power.

"He who is noble plans noble things, and on noble things he stands."
—Isaiah 32:8 ESV

3. Organize your priorities in a way that makes them easy to do:

- Prune and prioritize—*ask yourself, "How much time will these tasks and actions take?"*

- Start with time, not tasks: Peter Drucker—*if possible, give fifteen hours a week to your highest priority tasks.*

- DEAD: Delegate, Eliminate, Automate, Defer

Maintaining a flexible plan for your week: *schedule anything that needs to be scheduled.*

Managing Email and Workflow

Processing input is a *fundamental skill* of knowledge work.

Bad email and workflow practices:

- Using your email inbox as a to-do list

- Using your email inbox as a holding tank for major projects

"Clearing the decks tends to 'foster new, productive thinking that happens almost by itself' and 'increase our ability to handle greater engagement with the world.'"
—David Allen, *Ready for Anything: 52 Productivity Principles for Getting Things Done*

Making things easier when it comes to email and workflow:

1. Collect:

2. Process:

Three Big Rules of Processing Your Inbox

1. Process in order.
2. Process one item at a time.
3. Never put anything back into your inbox.

—David Allen, *Ready for Anything: Fifty-two Productivity
Principles for Getting Things Done*

The Questions of Processing

What is it?
- Trash
- Information
- Actionable
- Reference

What's the next action?
- The two-minute rule—do it right away
- Project and action lists
- Reference: files

Your email inbox is only for unprocessed items.

---

3. Organize and act:

Managing Projects and Actions—*The Project Plan*

A project is a multiple-action task.

Project list and action list (David Allen)

Project list: *all of your multistep initiatives*

Action list: *this is what you work from*

Weekly Plan: Next Action List

Organizing project plans: the four main categories of a project

1. **Purpose:** *Why are you doing this project?*

2. **Principles:** *High-level standards to guide the project*

3. **Actions:** *Upcoming steps for the project; includes brainstorming, new ideas, phases to make a path to project completion*

4. **Information:** *Project details to remember*

Actions: *Organizing your actions*

- Organizing actions by context (David Allen)

- Organizing actions by project (many executives)

- Organizing actions by area of your job (Matt Perman)

Find whatever works best for you!

The most important question: *What is on your list?*

Isaiah 32:8—*"Devise noble plans."*

Philippians 2:4—*"Look out for the interests of others."*

Daily Execution: Making Things Happen Every Day

How do you decide what to do in the moment?

Seven principles for making things happen every day:

1. Plan your day.

    • Start your day by looking at your weekly plan.
    • Jot down the three most important tasks.

2. Schedule your day at 70 percent capacity or less

    • Give yourself some space to get things done.

> *"Bulldozing through a ton of scheduled appointments and to-dos sets you up for frustration; the nature of most days will violate that expectation, and you'll miss some of the richest, most meaningful dimensions of living. Chances are also good that for much of that time you won't be putting first things first."*
> —Stephen Covey, *First Things First*

    • You operate better when you have space to think.

> *"When you think about it, absolutely everything anyone does starts with a thought. Because the quality of the thought has a large influence on the quality of the outcome, it makes sense to do what you can to think clearly. In a world in which technology provides the capacity to reach out and be reached anytime, anywhere, finding space to think clearly is more and more of a challenge. A lack of white space on one's calendar correlates with a lack of white space in one's brain."*
> —Scott Eblin, *The Next Level: What Insiders Know about Executive Success*

- The Ringing Effect

3. Consolidate your time into large chunks.

> *"To have small dribs and drabs of time at [your] disposal will not be sufficient even if the total is an impressive number of hours."*
> —Peter Drucker, *The Effective Executive*

> *"Most of the tasks of the executive require, for minimum effectiveness, a fairly large quantum of time. To spend in one stretch less than this minimum is sheer waste. One accomplishes nothing and has to begin all over again. . . . To be effective, every knowledge worker, and especially every executive, therefore needs to be able to dispose of time in fairly large chunks."*
> —Peter Drucker, *The Effective Executive*

4. Do one thing at a time.

- Concentration

> *"This is the 'secret' of those people who 'do so many things' and apparently so many difficult things. They do only one at a time. As a result, they need much less time in the end than the rest of us."*
> —Peter Drucker, *The Effective Executive*

5. See your day in terms of people and relationships first, not tasks.

6. Ask in everything, *"How can I build others up?"*

7. Utilize the key question in the moment: *What's Best Next?*

    - Dan Fuller: The core question of life is *What's Best Next?* (Eph. 5:15–17).
    - Alan Lakein: *What is the best use of my time right now?*

REFLECTION QUESTIONS

1. What outcomes are most important to you in life right now? Be sure to consider all areas of your life as you answer these questions.

2. Why do you think it's important to pray about your priorities and review your mission and vision on a consistent basis? How has this made a difference for you?

3. What are your top three to five priorities this week? How would you rank these priorities in order of importance?

4. What changes will you make to better manage your email and workflow as a result of what you learned in this session?

5. Up until this point, what kind of system or process were you using to manage your projects and actions? How was it working for you? Where do you need more help?

6. Author Matt Perman pointed out the difference between projects (large tasks) and actions (small tasks). Which tasks on your current to-do list are projects, and which ones are actions?

7. How does planning your week and scheduling your daily action steps affect your energy and work capacity?

8. **Read:** 1 Kings 6. Put yourself in Solomon's shoes with a little bit of imagination. What projects and action steps did Solomon have to think through as he rebuilt the temple?

9. How do you personally balance execution with focusing on outcomes instead of activities?

10. What reminders do you have in place to help you remember to put people first, not tasks, as you take action and execute daily?

Take Action: Follow these five steps for planning your week and the four steps to planning your day for one entire week and see how it makes a difference for you. Consider planning your week on Sunday evening or Monday morning, or whenever you begin your week.

---

5 Steps for Planning Your Week

1. Pray and review your mission and vision.
2. Define your priorities for the week by reflecting, reviewing your roles and goals, reviewing your project and action lists, reviewing your calendar, and getting creative about doing good.
3. Organize your priorities in a way that makes them easy to do. Separate the large activities from the small ones, prune and prioritize, schedule anything that needs to be scheduled, and do the small actions right away.
4. Don't skip planning, even when you are super busy.
5. Seize unplanned opportunities throughout the week.

---

4 Steps for Planning Your Day

1. Write down the three most important tasks you can accomplish today in light of your calendar and priorities.
2. Review your calendar and list any action this generates.
3. Review your priority list for the week and your actions list to ensure it is current, and identify any other priorities you need to have.
4. Write down any other things you need to do in light of upcoming meetings, appointments, and general other stuff you want to get done.

"Here's how I roll. I have a clear understanding every week of what needs to be done for the organization. I get up, I drink lots of coffee, and then do the things I think are most important. I'm not reacting to emails or calls but doing what I think has to happen. Which means the things that are important to the mission."
—Ben Peays, *The Gospel Coalition*

CLOSING PRAYER

- Ask God to help you this week by showing you where you need to take action and execute your priorities.
- Ask God to show you how you can do good in the world around you as you accomplish tasks and make progress on your projects.
- Pray for the perseverance to stick with this rhythm and routine of planning and executing so you can experience the benefits of completed tasks and extra capacity.
- Thank God for the opportunities he's given you to lead, plan, develop, and execute as you steward your gifts for the good of others and for his glory.

IN BETWEEN SESSIONS

EXERCISE ONE: Planning Your Week

Personal Reflection

Take time in personal reflection to think about the following questions.

➤ What do you *need* to do this week?

➤ What do you *want* to do this week?

Digging Deeper

Read the following passages and consider how these passages influence the way you plan your week.

Read: Philippians 2:1–10

➤ What stands out about this passage?

➤ How do you make sure your weekly plans are in the best interests of others and reflect the kind of life Jesus encourages us to live?

Read: Isaiah 32:1–8

➤ What stands out to you about the "righteous" and the "noble" in this passage?

➤ What are some righteous and noble actions you could take with how you plan your time this week?

Personal Action Steps

Consider action steps you can take as a result of what you read today.

➤ Get creative about doing good. Decide how you will do a few things for good in the following areas this week as you plan and prioritize what's necessary. Then go do them, either during scheduled time or during your free time.

- One action against injustice: _____
- Help someone in need: _____
- Do good for someone in my family, my neighborhood, my workplace, or my community: _____
- One action to fight against a large global problem: _____
  _____

Reflection and Prayer

Spend a few minutes in quiet personal reflection with God. Pray about whatever is on your mind as you consider the idea of executing your weekly plan. Or use these prayer suggestions as a guide:

- Tell God how you want to get this planning process right so you can free up your mind and time to do more good and glorify him.
- Ask God to help you organize your priorities in a way that makes them easy to do.
- Thank God for resources he's given to you through this material, and for your natural desire to organize, prioritize, and plan out your schedule. Thank God for the parts of this process that come easily and for the parts that are challenging, because of what the process is teaching you about yourself and about God.

_____
_____
_____
_____
_____
_____
_____
_____
_____
_____
_____

> *"No matter what kind of productivity approach you use, it is not going to work if you don't identify your most important priorities for the week."*
> —**Matt Perman, What's Best Next**

EXERCISE TWO: Managing Your Workflow

Personal Reflection

Take time in personal reflection to think about the following questions.

➤ How do you keep track of everything you want to do and need to do? Do you use a journal, a file system on your computer, or an online tool? Why does this tool work well for you? *Note: your email inbox is not meant to be the tool for your to-do lists and projects, and your brain can only hold so much information.*

➤ Which part of managing your workflow and project lists requires the most amount of your attention? How do you stay focused on these things?

Digging Deeper

Read the following passages and consider how these passages influence the way you manage your workflow and projects.

Read: Matthew 13:10–17

➤ Why does Jesus say he uses parables?

> ### The Parables of Jesus
>
> Since there was no printing press in Jesus' day, and parchment paper and ink were not always readily available, parables were the tools Jesus used to make an idea or lesson "stick." Without written reminders, if people could remember Jesus' stories, then they would remember his lessons too.

➤ How have parables made a difference in the way you understand the lessons of Jesus? Which one is most memorable to you?

Read: Matthew 25:14–30

➤ What lesson is Jesus trying to teach in this parable?

➤ How does this parable shape the way you decide what's best next?

Personal Action Steps

Consider one of these action steps you can take as a result of what you read today:

Action step one: the two-minute rule

The Two-Minute Rule

If you can do something in two minutes or less, do it right away.

➤ Try this rule as a tool to keep a consistent pace in your workflow. Look around you. Is there something you could take care of, clean up, schedule, or clear off your plate in the next two minutes? If so, do it. Practice this rule several times a day, before or after your routine breaks. However, if this rule is overwhelming to you, consider blocking off your time instead, and set time limits for checking email or for tasks that feel overwhelming. For example, one of my colleagues checks his email three times a day: once in the morning to scan for urgent updates, once after lunch to respond to emails, and once at the end of the day, again for updates.

Action step two: prioritize your projects

➤ Another action step you can take today is to organize your projects. This helps you maintain a consistent workflow. Not every project is a "right now" project. But you need a place for the ideas you generate regarding potential future projects. Here are four basic categories to help you prioritize your projects. List each one of your projects under their corresponding category.

How to Organize Projects

1. Weekly priority list (= this week)
2. Master projects list (= this quarter)
3. Master actions list (= this quarter)
4. Backburner (= someday/maybe)

Reflection and Prayer

Spend a few minutes in quiet personal reflection with God. Pray about whatever is on your mind as you consider ways to best navigate your workflow as you manage your projects. Or use these prayer suggestions as a guide:

- Ask God to help you do what *you* need to do when it comes to navigating your workflow and managing your projects. It can be easy to compare yourself to the way others do the same thing.
- Ask God to help you find the rhythm or routine that works best for you without feeling overwhelmed in the process. It can be easy to get lost in the weeks if you're focused on tasks instead of your priorities and the ideas you want to accomplish.
- Thank God for providing so many resources and tools that allow you to determine best practices regarding your individual preferences and your family calendar, as well as your workplace and community engagements.

"A good workflow process enables you to clear the decks for greater engagement and get things done with less friction and frustration."
—Matt Perman, *What's Best Next*

EXERCISE THREE: Making Things Happen

Personal Reflection

Take time in personal reflection to think about the following questions.

➤ How often do you fill your day to the brim with appointments and tasks? What does it feel like for you to maintain this kind of schedule?

➤ How do you decide what to do in the moment in order to get the most important things done without unnecessary distraction and friction?

Digging Deeper

Read the following passages and consider how these passages describe the various ways you can make things happen.

Read: Matthew 10

➤ According to this passage, how did the disciples know what's best next? What instructions or priorities were given to them by Jesus?

➤ How do you think you would have responded if you were one of the disciples with Jesus at this moment? Why?

Read: Mark 4:35–41

➤ What happened when Jesus prioritized rest while he was in the boat with the disciples?

➤ Has there ever been a time when you were prioritizing rest or time with your friends and family when you knew your coworkers or teammates were facing a "storm"? What allowed you to take time out in those moments?

Personal Action Steps

Consider action steps you can take as a result of what you read today.

➤ The two most essential questions in the Gospel-Driven Productivity method are:

1. What's best next? Or another way to ask this is: What's the best use of my time *now*?

2. How can I build others up in everything I do?

➤ Answer these two questions with simple responses that reflect exactly where you are *here and now* . . . and then go do them.

Reflection and Prayer

Spend a few minutes in quiet personal reflection with God. Pray about whatever is on your mind regarding the idea of making things happen as you execute your plans and priorities on a daily and weekly basis. Or use these prayer suggestions as a guide:

- Tell God where you need to focus the most: on prioritizing your weekly plans or taking daily action.
- Ask God to show you how to make the most of your tasks and projects so you can be present for what really matters in your life.
- Thank God for caring about the work you do and what matters most in your life. Express your gratitude for the ways God has guided you in the process of putting methods and tools into place so you can focus on what's best next.

"The more one can concentrate time, effort, and resources, the greater the number and diversity of tasks one can actually perform. . . . [Effective executives] concentrate—their own time and energy as well as that of their organization—on doing one thing at a time, and on doing first things first."
—Peter Drucker, quoted in *What's Best Next*

EXPLORING ADDITIONAL RESOURCES

Take some time to explore the additional resources recommended in *What's Best Next* session 6:

David Allen, *Getting Things Done*

Stephen Covey, "Quadrant II Organizing: The Process of Putting Things First" and "The Perspective of the Week," chapters 4 and 8 in *First Things First*

Yearly Planning: http://www.whatsbestnext.com/2010/12/advice-for-entering -the-new-year-the-yearly-review/

Checking Email: http://www.whatsbestnext.com/2009/02/what-if-the-post-office -delivered-mail-the-way-most-of-us-check-email/.

"How to Get Your Email Inbox to Zero Everyday": https://www.whatsbestnext .com/2016/06/get-email-inbox-zero-every-day-updated/

Checking Email: "How to Get the Mail": http://www.whatsbestnext.com/2008/ 10/how-to-get-the-mail/

G. Lynne Snead and Joyce Wycoff, "Organizing Your Time and the Flood of Information," section 2 in *To Do, Doing, Done*

Gina Trapani, "Hack 22: Make Your To-Do List Doable," chapter 3 in *Upgrade Your Life: The Lifehacker Guide to Working Smarter, Faster, Better*

"Thoughts on Daily To-Do Lists": http://www.whatsbestnext.com/2009/08/thoughts -on-daily-to-do-lists/

Lynne Snead and Joyce Wycoff, *To Do, Doing, Done: A Creative Approach to Managing Projects and Effectively Finishing What Matters Most*

Scott Berkun, *The Art of Project Management*

Nancy Mingus, *Alpha Teach Yourself Project Management in 24 Hours*

Kelly Goto and Emily Cotlet, *Web ReDesign 2.0: Workflow that Works*

June Cohen, *The Unusually Useful Web Book*

PREPARATION FOR NEXT SESSION

As you reflect on what God is teaching you through this session, read or review part 6: chapters 19–22 of *What's Best Next* by Matt Perman. Also in preparation for the last session, you will want to read part 7: chapters 23–25.

NOTES

LIVING THIS OUT

Let us be on the watch for opportunities out of usefulness; let us go about the world with our ears and our eyes open, ready to avail ourselves of every occasion for doing good; let us not be content till we are useful, but make this the main design and ambition of our lives.
—Charles Spurgeon, *Counsel for Christian Workers*

INTRODUCTION

The Results

So this is it. The last session of the *What's Best Next* study guide, and the place where I tell you that the intended results of Gospel-Driven Productivity are a *sense of greater fulfillment* and *peace of mind in your vocation*, as well as a *wider concern regarding productivity* in your organizations, in our society as a whole, and in the Great Commission. That's right, Gospel-Driven Productivity ultimately leads to greater concern and care for global missions. While it might be tempting then to shift all of our productivity efforts to taking the gospel to the ends of the earth, I'm here to remind you that spreading the gospel and transforming the world begins with effective productivity in our everyday lives. Therefore, the importance of your work rises far above personal satisfaction and extends to global transformation for the glory of God.

Because productivity is a biblical command that inspires us to seek the good of others, our role as Christians is to pray and seek the good of society as a whole. This requires us to focus equal amounts of energy on increasing our own effectiveness, making our organizations more productive, and making our society more effective so that life can be improved on a global scale. The bottom line of Gospel-Driven Productivity is to understand that God calls us to use productivity practices for the good of others and the sake of the poor. This doesn't just mean giving money to help those in need (although this is important too), but we are also to think about how to take the best actions on behalf of the poor and create productive plans to make those actions happen. This doesn't necessarily mean selling everything you own and moving to Africa to be a missionary. It means recognizing the important opportunity you have each and every day to serve God at work, in your home, at school, in your neighborhood, and in your church community.

Living out Gospel-Driven Productivity happens when you begin to see that everything you do, in *all* areas of your life, is a means of serving God and others. But it is important to acknowledge that our productivity does not happen without suffering, because some measure of frustration and suffering is inherent in all of our work due to the fall. There is no way around the suffering. Yet God still works all things together for good and for his purpose, including our suffering. This is the heart of Gospel-Driven Productivity: *to show the greatness of Jesus Christ by effectively doing good for others in every situation, including our times of suffering.* My hope for you moving forward is that you practice the discipline of personal productivity so you can increase your effectiveness in work and life for the good of others and the glory of God.

THINK ABOUT IT

➤ How does personal productivity lead to greater peace of mind and more fulfillment for you?

-or-

➤ How do you play a key part in spreading the gospel and changing the world in your everyday personal and professional life?

VIDEO TEACHING NOTES

Productivity in Organizations and Society

Our aim should be to increase our ability to do good for others.

We need to broaden our view of productivity:

- Life

- Work

- Organizations

- Society

"Christian love . . . disposes a person to be public-spirited. A man of a right spirit is not a man of narrow and private views, but is greatly interested and concerned for the good for the community to which he belongs, and particularly of the city or village in which he resides, and for the true welfare of the society of which he is a member."
—Jonathan Edwards, *Charity and Its Fruits*

> **"Seek the welfare of the city where I have sent you into exile, and pray to the LORD on its behalf, for in its welfare you will find your welfare."**
> **—Jeremiah 29:7 ESV**

The creation mandate: *To serve culture*

We are sojourners and exiles on the earth (1 Peter 1:1, 17 and Heb. 11:13).

The law drives us to the gospel.

Definitive sanctification—*we are made alive to righteousness, and die to sin, so we can do good.*

> **"Whatever the post of honor or influence we may be placed in, we should show that, in it, we are solicitous for the good of the public, so that the world may be better for our living in it, and that, when we are gone, it may be said of us, as it was so nobly said of David, that we 'served our generation by the will of God.'"**
> **—Jonathan Edwards, *Charity and Its Fruits***

Seeking the good of our organizations:

> *"Modern society depends for its functioning if not for its survival, on the effectiveness of large-scale organizations, on their performance and results, and on their values, standards, and self-demands."*
> —Peter Drucker, *The Effective Executive*

Individual effectiveness is a building block toward organizational effectiveness.

Understanding management and leadership to truly serve our organizations:

1. Become more effective ourselves

2. Know how to run organizations more effectively

Good management and leadership are the results of loving others.

Be diligent in seeking to learn:

- Marcus Buckingham's *First Break All the Rules: What the World's Greatest Managers Do Differently*

- John Kotter's "What Leaders Really Do," *Harvard Business Review*

- Marcus Buckingham's *The One Thing You Need to Know*

We need to understand economics to make society productive:

- Thomas Sowell's *Basic Economics*—the foundational principles of economics

- The Centrality of Freedom

The Greatest Cause in the World: World Missions

> "And those that are possessed of the spirit of Christian charity are of a more enlarged spirit still, for they are concerned, not only for the thrift of the community, but for the welfare of the church of God, and of all the people of God individually."
> —Jonathan Edwards, *Charity and Its Fruits*

> "For its own soul the church needs to be involved in missions. We will not know God in his full majesty until we know him moving triumphantly among the nations."
> —John Piper, *Don't Waste Your Life*

The Christian spirit has a heart for those who do not yet know Christ.

> "I endure everything for the sake of the elect, that they also may obtain the salvation that is in Christ Jesus with eternal glory."
> —2 Timothy 2:10 ESV

God's global call: Make the gospel known.

- We are to make disciples of all nations and take the gospel to the ends of the earth—Matthew 28:18–20; Acts 1:8.

> *"The message of biblical Christianity is not 'God loves me, period' . . . the message of biblical Christianity is 'God loves me so that I might make him—his ways, his salvation, his glory, his greatness—known among all nations.'"*
> —David Platt, *Radical: Taking Back Your Faith from the American Dream*

Social good as part of missions

Four reasons God calls us to care holistically for people:

1. The example of Jesus (Matt. 4:23; Luke 24:19)

2. The command to love our neighbor as ourselves (Matt. 22:36–39)

3. Meeting people's needs is part of righteousness . . . and mercy (Mic. 6:8; Matt. 23:23; Matt. 9:13, 12:7; Hos. 6:6; James 1:27; Jer. 22:15–17; 1 John 3:16–17; Matt. 25:33–46).

4. We are to work against the unjust social structures that lead to oppression (Isa. 1:17; 58:5; Job 24:1–21; 31:16–23).

> *"Give justice to the weak and the fatherless;*
> *maintain the right of the afflicted and the destitute.*
> *Rescue the weak and the needy;*
> *deliver them from the hand of the wicked."*
> **—Psalm 82:3–4 ESV**
>
> *"Wilberforce and the band of abolitionists knew that a private faith*
> *that did not act in the face of oppression was no faith at all."*
> **—Chuck Colson**

The global call is based on both creation and redemption.

God's call is that we make a large dent in helping the poor.

How do we pursue Gospel-Driven Productivity as we serve God?

1. Helping the poor is a partnership.

   • Steve Corbett and Brian Fikkert's *When Helping Hurts*

   • Ditch the superiority complex.

2. Carve out deliberate time to take a few steps against large global problems.

   - Clay Shirky's *Cognitive Surplus*

   - Pray focused prayers.

   - Get involved: Kiva, etc.

3. Good productivity makes you more effective for the global fight.

   - God works through our work to serve the world and bring transformation to the world.

How making the most of the time right where we are transforms the world

Paul's writing in Ephesians 5: *Walking as light—following God's ethical teaching*

"Take no part in the unfruitful works of darkness, but instead expose them."
—Ephesians 5:11 ESV

"But when anything is exposed by the light, it becomes visible."
—Ephesians 5:13 ESV

"It is even possible (after all, it happened to you!) for light
to turn the thing it shines upon into light also."
—J. B. Phillips, paraphrase of Ephesians 5:8

He who is wise wins souls (Prov. 11:30).

Let your light shine before others (Matt. 5:16).

Scripture makes a connection between productivity and the advancement of the gospel.

The world changes when institutions change, but institutions change when people change.

> *"Want to change the world? Push everyone you know to work within their intersection. Mentor people to realize their genuine interests, skills, and to capitalize on even the smallest opportunities that surround them. When it comes to your own career, make every decision with a constant eye for work in the intersection."*
> —Scott Belsky, "Finding Your Work Sweet Spot"
>
> *"Please take yourself and your creative pursuits seriously. Your ideas must be treated with respect because their importance truly does extend beyond your own interests. Every living person benefits from a world that is enriched with ideas made whole—ideas that are made to happen through your passion, commitment, self-awareness, and informed pursuit."*
> —Scott Belsky, Making Ideas Happen: Overcoming the Obstacles between Vision and Reality

To change the world, first change your world. Be a positive influence for good.

Your purpose: show the greatness of Jesus by doing good for others.

Be creative, competent, audacious in doing good for the world.

> *"Let us be on the watch for opportunities of usefulness; let us go about the world with our ears and eyes open, ready to avail ourselves of every occasion for doing good; let us not be content 'til we are useful, but make this the main design and ambition of our lives."*
> —Charles Spurgeon, *The Soul Winner*

REFLECTION QUESTIONS

1. In what ways does your individual effectiveness influence your personal life and your work life?

2. How do you contribute to the overall effectiveness of your organization? How do you call forth the best in the people around you?

3. How do you contribute to the overall effectiveness of society?

4. What sources do you read to stay on top of the latest news regarding leadership, management, and economics? As Matt Perman pointed out, this knowledge is crucial in leading and loving well in our organizations and in society.

5. How does Christianity teach that we are to be concerned for the whole person, not just the spiritual dimension? Share examples that come to mind.

6. **Read:** 1 Timothy 6:17–19. How does this passage inspire you to move toward action with your resources and your influence?

7. How do you currently use your productivity practices for the sake of the poor? Can you name other individuals or organizations who are doing this well?

8. God calls us to serve right where we are *and* beyond, and he gives us the advanced technology to do so in our modern age. How has technology enabled you to serve where you are and beyond?

9. **Read:** Proverbs 3. What stands out to you about the two descriptions of wisdom in this passage: living well in this world and pointing people to God?

10. How have you experienced *suffering* in your vocation?

Take Action: Research five different ways you can contribute to fighting global poverty or spread the gospel to unreached people groups with your time, energy, talents, and resources. List those options here, then take action on at least one of these ways today:

1. _____
2. _____
3. _____
4. _____
5. _____

> *"Be creative, competent, and audacious in doing all the good you can for the world, in big and small ways, both right where you are and in the cause of global good, to the glory of God, according to your gifts and abilities. Use technology and productivity practices to do that. And, as you do this in the power of the gospel, the world will change."*
> —Matt Perman, *What's Best Next*

CLOSING PRAYER

- Ask God to help you see how your individual productivity contributes to overall effectiveness in your organization.
- Ask God to show you how your individual and your organization's effectiveness give you the opportunity to contribute to fighting larger global issues.
- Pray for clarity regarding which particular global issue you can most effectively address in your current work situation, or in your personal circumstances.
- Thank God that all things work together for good, according to his purposes, even when you experience frustration and suffering in your life.

IN BETWEEN SESSIONS

EXERCISE ONE: Expanding Our View of Productivity

Personal Reflection

Take time in personal reflection to think about the following questions.

The Four Dimensions of Productivity

1. Personal life
2. Work life
3. Organizations
4. Society

➤ As Christians, we are to seek effectiveness in all of these areas of productivity. Which one is most natural for you to focus on in regard to effectiveness? Why?

➤ Which one is the most challenging to focus on? Why?

Digging Deeper

Read the following passages and consider how these passages influence your expanded view of productivity.

Read: Jeremiah 29:7

➤ What does God command his people to do in this passage?

➤ What does it look like for you to seek peace and prosperity in your city, your neighborhood, and your home?

Read: Galatians 2:10

➤ What does it mean to remember the poor, and how are you doing this in your own life?

➤ How would you characterize the "poor" in your world?

Personal Action Steps

Consider action steps you can take as a result of what you read today.

➤ In order to grow in your effective management and leadership, Matt Perman suggests reading *Basic Economics: A Citizen's Guide to the Economy* by Thomas Sowell. Buy, download, or check this book out of the library and read it this week. Take notes and discuss your thoughts with a friend or coworker.

Reflection and Prayer

Spend a few minutes in quiet personal reflection with God. Pray about whatever is on your mind as you consider your expanded view of productivity. Or use these prayer suggestions as a guide:

- Tell God how you want to give him the glory in every area of your life, including the way your personal productivity affects the greater good of humanity.
- Ask God to help you prioritize the poor and those living in poverty above the attention of experiencing little luxuries in your own life.
- Thank God for resources he's given you as you seek to do good for others and bring glory to his name in all that you do.

> *"Personal effectiveness has an impact on the spirit and culture of an organization, creating an environment that calls forth the best from everyone. This raises the sights of everybody and creates an environment that calls forth their best. This is good for everyone individually and for the organization."*
> —Matt Perman, *What's Best Next*

EXERCISE TWO: The Greatest Cause

Personal Reflection

Take time in personal reflection to think about the following questions.

➤ We make the most of our time by pursuing wisdom—knowing how to live well in the world and pointing people to Christ. How does your life reflect this kind of wisdom?

➤ Author Scott Belsky says that we change the world by operating in our vocational "sweet spot"—the intersection of our interests, skills, and opportunities—and pushing everyone else we know to do the same. How is this true for you? And how have you encouraged others to realize the opportunities around them?

Digging Deeper

Read the following passages and consider how these passages influence the way you contribute to the greatest cause.

Read: Mark 12:35–40

➤ Why is Jesus so bothered in this passage?

➤ What would Jesus say about the way you are living your life right now? Would he say that you are caring about important matters, or that you are living like a "scribe" who acts like a hypocrite?

Read: James 1:26–27

➤ What does it mean to be "religious"?

➤ According to this passage, how well are you doing at being "religious"?

Personal Action Steps

Consider action steps you can take as a result of what you read today.

➤ Matt Perman says, "We need to start thinking about how to complete the Great Commission. At the center of our thinking needs to be the recognition that productivity is one of the chief means through which we transform society and the gospel spreads—both here and beyond."

The Great Commission

"Then Jesus came to them and said, 'All authority in heaven and on earth has been given to me. Therefore go and make disciples of all nations, baptizing them in the name of the Father and of the Son and of the Holy Spirit, and teaching them to obey everything I have commanded you. And surely, I am with you always, to the very end of the age.'"

—Matthew 28:18–20

➤ The Great Commission never changes, but the expression of it may change in our lives according to our life stage, our roles, and therefore, our calling. List two or three actions you can take this week to live out the Great Commission right where you are, in your everyday personal and professional life:

_____

_____

_____

Reflection and Prayer

Spend a few minutes in quiet personal reflection with God. Pray about whatever is on your mind as you consider the greatest cause of Gospel-Driven Productivity. Or use these prayer suggestions as a guide:

- Ask God to show you what it looks like for you to do good for others—the greatest cause—in your everyday life.
- Ask God to give you opportunities to put your desires and good intentions into actions and good deeds.
- Thank God for inviting you to be a part of the crucial work he is doing in the world, by allowing you to start right where you are.

"Want to change the world? Push everyone you know to work within their intersection. Mentor people to realize their genuine interests, skills and to capitalize on even the smallest opportunities that surround them. When it comes to your own career, make every decision with a constant eye for work in the intersection. A career of 'work with intention' is the kind that moves industries forward. Do it for yourself and for the rest of us."
—Scott Belsky, *Making Ideas Happen*

EXERCISE THREE: Productivity in a Fallen World

Personal Reflection

Take time in personal reflection to think about the following questions.

➤ How have you attempted to overcome suffering and frustration in your work life?

➤ Why do you think so many of us get to the end of the day only to find ourselves frustrated by failing to accomplish what we intended?

Digging Deeper

Read the following passages and consider how these passages describe responses to living and working in a fallen world.

Read: Genesis 3

➤ How does it feel to know that doing the right thing will not always lead to success, and that frustration or some level of suffering will always be a part of the work we do because of the fall?

Read: Romans 8:28–39

➤ How has God used your suffering for good?

➤ According to this passage, what do you think it means to be "more than conquerors"? And what does it specifically look like for you in your current context or circumstances to be "more than a conqueror"?

Personal Action Steps

Consider action steps you can take as a result of what you read today.

➤ Take note of how you will put these ways of responding to suffering into practice this week.

1. *Minimize* your suffering—internal and external—to the extent you can.
   _____

2. *Embrace* suffering for the good of others. _____
   _____

3. *Recognize* the great and unique privilege it is to suffer in faith for God's glory.
   _____

Reflection and Prayer

Spend a few minutes in quiet personal reflection with God. Pray about whatever is on your mind regarding the idea of what it means to be productive in a fallen world. Or use these prayer suggestions as a guide:

- Tell God how you are feeling frustrated or where you are experiencing suffering in your life. God already knows these things, but he longs to hear them directly from you.
- Ask God to give you a glimpse of the purpose in your suffering, so you can hang on with hope.
- Thank God for caring about your suffering and your frustration. Also thank God for being your refuge in the midst of your suffering. And thank him that he promises to work all things together for good.

"Biblical productivity is productivity through suffering. If we respond in faith, times of hardship and low productivity can become our times of greatest productivity. For God turns all things good."
—Matt Perman, *What's Best Next*

EXPLORING ADDITIONAL RESOURCES

Take some time to explore the additional resources recommended in *What's Best Next* session 7:

Marcus Buckingham and Curt Coffman, *First Break All the Rules: What the World's Greatest Managers Do Differently*

Peter Drucker, *Managing the Nonprofit Organization*

Peter Drucker, *The Practice of Management*

Marcus Buckingham, *The One Thing You Need to Know*

John Kotter, "What Leaders Really Do, *Harvard Business Review*, December 2001 (reprint), http://www.hbr.org/2001/12/what-leaders-really-do/ar/1.

Rudy Giuliani, *Leadership*

Stephen Covey, *Principle-Centered Leadership*

Thomas Sowell, *Basic Economics*

Milton Friedman, *Free to Choose*

F. A. Hayek, *The Road to Serfdom*

Doug Bandow, *Beyond Good Intentions: A Biblical View of Politics*

John Piper, *The Supremacy of God in Missions*

David Platt, *Radical: Taking Your Faith Back from the American Dream*

Vishal Mangalwadi and Ruth Mangalwadi, *The Legacy of William Carey: A Model for the Transformation of Culture*

Tim Keller, *Ministries of Mercy*

Steve Corbett and Brian Fikkert, *When Helping Hurts*

Peter Greer and Phil Smith, *The Poor Will Be Glad: Joining the Revolution to Lift the World out of Poverty*

Bjorn Lomborg, *How to Spend $50 Billion to Make the World a Better Place*

Gary Haugen, *Good News about Injustice: A Witness of Courage in a Hurting World*

Timothy Keller, *Every Good Endeavor: Connecting Your Work to God's Work*

Paul Rude, *Significant Work: Discover the Extraordinary Worth of What You Do Every Day*

Tom Nelson, *Work Matters: Connecting Sunday Worship to Monday Work*

CLOSING

As you reflect on what God is teaching you through this session, read or review part 7: chapters 23–25 of *What's Best Next* by Matt Perman.

NOTES

CLOSING WORDS

If we want to live a productive life, we must look to God to define what productivity means for us in every season, for God is what matters most. With this perspective, we can recognize the significance of things we do each and every day, because they are means by which we serve him and others. We determine *what's best next* by asking ourselves, first, what we can do for the good of others. When we serve others with our productivity, we also serve God and make his name known in the world.

Let me close by saying this: In our current era of massive overload and incredible opportunity, we need to practice these four steps to be most effective, to stay on track, and to lead and manage our lives effectively:

1. Define
2. Architect
3. Reduce
4. Execute

As we follow these steps, we will take our faith into the world, shine the light of the gospel, and contribute to the transformation of the world through global missions and global good. This is our calling. May you continue to show the greatness of Jesus by increasing your effectiveness, by organizing your life around Gospel-Driven Productivity, and by doing good for others.

—*Matt Perman*